The Ratan Tata Way

The Ratan Tata *Way*

Complete Biography & Success Secrets

A.K. GANDHI
VINOD SHARMA

Published by
PRABHAT PRAKASHAN PVT. LTD.
4/19 Asaf Ali Road,
New Delhi-110002 (INDIA)
e-mail: prabhatbooks@gmail.com

ISBN 978-93-5562-408-6
THE RATAN TATA WAY: COMPLETE BIOGRAPHY & SUCCESS SECRETS
by A.K. Gandhi *&* Vinod Sharma

Edition
2024

Price
₹ 450 (Rupees Four Hundred Fifty Only)

Printed at
SS Japan Arts, Delhi

Dedicated to the father of

TATA Group

'Bharat Ratna' awardee

Shri J.R.D.TATA

who gave a new definition and direction

to entrepreneurship

Author's Note

The Tata Group is synonymous with Indian entrepreneurial success and nation-building. As one of India's most respected corporate leaders, Ratan Tata has been an inseparable part of this iconic legacy.

In writing 'The Ratan Tata Way', my aim has been to provide a comprehensive portrayal of the man behind the empire. This book is not just a chronological account of his life and the Tata group's history, but also an exploration of the values, principles and leadership philosophy that have shaped Ratan Tata's extraordinary journey.

Having closely followed his career, I have attempted to distill the key influences, life experiences and thought processes that motivated his actions and decisions as he skillfully lead the Tata firms into the 21st century. The book delves into his formative years and the challenges he faced in reviving and expanding the group after taking over as chairman in 1991.

Ratan Tata's vision transcended just business - he revolutionised the group's management ethos and pioneered progressive human resource policies. His commitment to society is exemplified by the group's philanthropic initiatives in education, healthcare and rural empowerment.

Through extensive research, interviews and by examining his public statements, I have endeavored to provide an authentic understanding of Ratan Tata's mind and the 'Tata Way' of conducting business with integrity and ethics.

It is my sincere hope that this book serves as a worthy tribute to an iconic leader who epitomises the virtues of humility, perseverance and moral courage against all odds.

– A.K. Gandhi

❑

Contents

Complete
Biography

Family Background

The Parsi community is believed to have lived in Persia (present-day Iran) hundreds of years ago. Their people gradually spread to all the countries of the world based on trade and industry. In the same sequence, the Parsis also arrived in India centuries ago. Despite being spread across many regions of the world, their number is limited. They are considered particularly the worshippers of fire, but they also worship the sun, moon, and air. In the old days, the Parsi community gave special emphasis to archery, horse riding, and character-building. Changes in many areas were inevitable over time. Nevertheless, their perseverance on the purity of community and character is more or less still intact. As a community inclined towards preserving their heritage they do not encourage marriage outside their own societies, even if they married in close relationships, so that the purity of the caste could be preserved. This taboo is still present to a great extent. Even mentally, Parsis are very strong and their behaviour is dignified. Their performance in knowledge and science and their field of work is generally commendable.

The Parsis have created a special place for themselves in Indian society. They have earned the respect they truly deserve, and have played an important role not only in the industrial world but also in contemporary social activities. Along with making a significant contribution to the economic development of the country, they have discharged the national and social commitments with efficiency and integrity. Despite having minority status, they have not redeemed it for political-economic benefit but have focused on creating opportunities for their growth through diligence and dedication. This is an important characteristic and quality that they possess.

Navsari is also one of the oldest towns in Gujarat. Centuries ago, a group of Parsis came and settled here. For some time, the region was also under the influence of Parsis, later it was taken over by the Muslim invaders. At the time of the country's independence in 1947, this area was under the princely state of Baroda. Navsari has been the home of a sizeable class of Parsis. Dadabhai Naoroji, who was elected as a member of the British Parliament during the British rule, was also born in Navsari.

Navsari was also the residence of Nausherwanji Tata, father of Jamsetji Tata, the founder of the Tata Gharana. Jamsetji Tata's birthplace is Navsari. Today their residence is preserved as a memorial.

Jamsetji's father Nausherwanji belonged to the branch of the Parsi community, which was involved in hieratic work. His ancestors did the same work for many generations. Therefore, they were also counted among the respected classes of the society. With the changing times, the uneasiness of change started in all societies. The Tata family of the Parsi community also could not remain untouched by this. Nausherwanji was the first man in the Tata family who instead of sticking to centuries-old tradition and values, thought of going ahead and achieving something new. As a result, he decided to make business his field of work and means of livelihood.

The town Navsari was quite backward at that time, so to fulfil his dream, he found Bombay perfectly suitable and left Navsari for Bombay. He started his work with business and banking. Although this was a new and unfamiliar area for him, he still progressed with steady steps. As the experience grew, his thinking also got a new direction and he took a concrete decision for the future that they had to lead their future generations in this direction only.

His only son Jamset was in Navsari during this period. To give a practical form to his dream, he also called him to Bombay, so that he could be raised properly and with experience in the proper business environment, he could also get business skills, which would prove helpful in shaping his future.

❑

Jamsetji Tata

The leading man of the Indian industrial world, Yugdrashta Jamset Nausherwanji Tata, was born on March 3, in Navsari in a family of Parsi Priests. He is called the father of Indian industry.He was the only son of his father and his childhood was spent in Navsari.

When Jamsetji was 13, his father started an export business in Bombay. He made his debut in Bombay at the age of 14. According to Parsi tradition, he was married at the age of 16 to Hirabai (10 years). Nausherwanji wanted his son to get higher education, so at the age of 17, he was admitted to Elphinstone College. After a few years he completed his college education as a 'Green Scholar' (equivalent to graduation). His attachment to literature and books continued throughout his life. After completing his education, his father enrolled him into his business and taught him the technicalities of operation.

In 1859, his father sent him on a business trip to Hong Kong, where he worked to open a branch of his family firm and was busy with other related tasks. He lived there till 1863.

Debut in the Industrial Field

At the age of 29, he started a personal trading firm in 1868 with a capital of ₹ 2100. Through this, Jamsetji and his partners got the contract to supply some military equipment abroad. There was a sufficient amount of profit in this which inspired him to start his work in the field of textiles. In partnership with some of his friends, he bought an old oil mill in Bombay in 1869 and converted it into a textile (cloth manufacturing) factory. He undertook the task of managing it himself and within a few years he changed it into a working factory. Two years later he sold it to a textile businessman at profit. He named it 'Alexandra Cotton Mill'.

In 1872, Jamsetji once again turned towards England. This time his aim was to study the industry there, especially the textile business in Lancashire. He was keen to develop the Indian textile industry.

At that time there were about a dozen textile mills in Bombay and it was considered a suitable place for textile mills. But contrary to this thinking, Jamsetji chose Nagpur, in central India to set up his factory. Thus, they also got the benefit of the railway facilities established in that area during that time. While choosing Nagpur city, he kept in mind three main facts - cotton production, railway facilities and fuel and the water supply situation.

In 1874, he started 'The Central Indian Spinning, Weaving And Manufacturing Company' with a capital of 15,00,000 investing capital along with his friends. After declaring Queen Victoria as Queen of India on January 1, 1877, the 'Empires Mill' was started in Nagpur.

The yarn cloth mill of Nagpur also worked as a laboratory for Jamsetji. Here he focused on every single detail of its development. Special focus was given on new experiments of technology and labour welfare. Quality of the fabric was also improved by substituting the most advanced American machinery of that era. He made new facilities like the pension fund in 1886 and accident compensation in 1895 for his workers. In this way he surpassed his competitors.

Encouraged by his primary successes, in 1886 only he thought of purchasing a defamed ailing mill. At the age of 47 he accepted the challenge of turning this sick mill into a healthy one. This mill, named 'Swadeshi Cotton Mill' on the lines of the Swadeshi movement, was mainly supported by Indian share-holders. He invested in it willingly. But later on, some situations were such that even after two years the mill could not declare dividends. Due to some reasons and rumours, prices of the share fell. The name of 'Tata' was at stake. When the banks also refused to give loans, Jamsetji collected capital by selling some shares of his Family Trust and Empires Mill and invested it in the indigenous cotton mill. This had the desired effect and the stock prices rose. He provided the best services of his best minds and skilled employees to the Swadeshi Cotton Mill and within a few years transformed it into a high-grade textile mill. Soon the fabric manufactured in it began to get exported to China, Korea, Japan and the Middle East.

When Jamsetji realized that the bulk of the company's profit was spent in paying the freight for water transportation of goods from Bombay to China and the Japan branches he took the initiative to change the situation. At that time, this waterway was predominantly monopolized by three companies, which always kept their rates high. So Jamsetji turned to a Japanese steam navigation company called 'Nippon Yusen Kaisha' to facilitate cheap transportation. Monopoly companies opposed this, but Jamsetji fought it out and emerged victorious. In June 1896, these companies were forced to reduce their freight to a reasonable and competitive level.

Jamsetji was fully aware that the industrial revolution is a fundamental requirement for industrial success, so he was determined to use the advanced technology and methods prevalent in the industrial sector. At that time, the work of increasing the network of railways and telegraph to connect different regions of India was going on. The Tata group made meaningful use of it in expanding its industrial empire.

Entry into the Iron and Steel Industry

During his stay in England Jamsetji had decided that he would definitely establish an Iron and Steel industry in India. In view of the circumstances of that time this thought was a courageous step. India's then British government was also not interested in developing big businesses in India. Therefore, the policies of the government were automatically a road block. But Jamsetji was unstoppable to embody his imagination.

In 1901, Jamsetji focused on the Indian steel industry which was at its primary stage at that time and produced a small amount of steel. In this work he took the help of British and American surveyors. The main name among them is that of an American Charles Page Perin, who spent many years in India for the Geological Survey of India to find iron deposits. Later on, a few Indian surveyors also supported him. He travelled to European countries and America for technical advice and information of steel making. He wanted to undertake iron refining on a large scale so he invested a substantial amount of money on this project. Before Jamsetji's plan could take shape, he died in Germany in 1904. He had two sons to decorate, cherish, develop and fulfil his incomplete dreams, elder son Dorabji and the younger son Ratan and to support both of them Jamsetji's cousin R.D. Tata was present. Before he died, he had expressed his wish to his cousin R.D. Tata, son Dorab and other close relatives to carry forward the work he had started. If they could not do so then at least should preserve to continue the work done so far.

Jamsetji's dream of steel making came true when the Tata Steel and Iron Company was established in 1907 at Sakchi, 150 miles west of Calcutta. This place was suitable for raw materials, coal, water supply and transportation, so the company grew rapidly. On February 16, 1912, the first steel ingot was produced from the Sakchi plant in a happy and positive atmosphere. Today it is a major steel industry in the country. The imagination Jamsetji had for his steel city was given full respect in the making of Jamshedpur (Sakchi).

Construction of the Taj Mahal Hotel

Jamsetji built India's best hotel the Taj Mahal Hotel in Bombay. A sizeable amount of money was spent in its construction. His purpose behind its construction was to promote tourism by attracting travellers to India. He himself bought the furnishings of the hotel during his travels. The hotel was well equipped with all the facilities in line with European standards of that time. In this, all necessary arrangements were made, including a soda and ice factory, washing and polishing machines, laundry, elevators and electric generators. It was inaugurated in 1903. At that time, it was the first building in Bombay which was lighted. It had American fans and Turkey styled bathrooms. English butlers were appointed for the kitchen. Overall, the hotel had all the facilities that were present in the world's best-known hotels.

Jamsetji's Public Welfare Works

Jamshetji was deeply connected with the rites of benevolence. For this, in 1892, he established the J.N. Tata Trust. He established a fund for higher education. Under this, he sent deserving students abroad for higher education. Under this scheme, many of India's early engineers, surgeons, physicians, barristers and ICS officers were benefited.

In 1898, he presented his fourteen buildings, a large sum of money and four properties for the establishment of the

Post Graduate Institute for Scientific Research. Although his dream could not be fulfilled during his lifetime due to the high-handedness of the British Government, but his sons fulfilled it after his death. Thus in 1911, the institute was established in Bangalore, which was a joint collaboration of Tata, Government of India and Government of Mysore. Initially it had only three major departments — General and Applied Chemistry, Electro Technology Chemistry and Organic Chemistry. Later, many other departments were added to it periodically.

Like Tata Steel, Jamshedpur, the Indian Institute, Bangalore served as a centre from which later many other branches—Central Food and Technological Research Institute, Mysore; Lac Research Institute, Ranchi; National Aeronautical Laboratory, Bangalore bloomed. It also contributed to the establishment and development of many other institutions.

Endowed with Vision and Intuition

Jamsetji will also be remembered for his vision, intuition and for imbibing and implementing new ideas and fantasies. He used it not only to develop his business but also to improve the lives of his compatriots. He gave importance to innovation and was the first person to use rubber tires in the wagon. He was the first automobile driver in Bombay who donated generously for essential works. He was steeped in high social ideals and made new arrangements for labour facilities and their welfare in the field of labour and introduced new rules, which would not have been in the imagination of anyone else. Those reforms were implemented abroad after several decades. Numerous reforms came into existence only after multifarious movements. The whole country still respects him and remembers him with gratitude.

On January 7, 1965, the Indian Postal and Telegraph Department commenced a postage stamp in honour of Jamsetji. It shows the gratitude of the country for his services in the industrialization of the country.

❑

Sir Dorabji Tata

Dorabji was the elder son of Jamsetji Tata, who, after his death, raised care of his legacy and took it to new heights. His younger brother Sir Ratan Tata and Jamsetji's cousin Ratan Dadabhai Tata gave full support in this task. It was his optimism and strong will power that helped the Tata Group overcome every difficulty and he managed to take the company to great acclaim by giving form to his father's dreams.

Dorabji was born in 1859 and got his primary education at the Proprietary High School in Bombay. He was then sent to England. At the age of 18, he attended Gonville and Caius College in Cambridge. He also performed well in sports while studying at Cambridge and won several awards in cricket and football. Dorabji returned to India in 1879 and enrolled at St. Xavier's College, Bombay. After completion of his education, he started his work as a journalist at the '*Bombay Gazette*'. Gradually he became interested in his father's business and in 1884 he entered the ancestral business. He was accommodated in the cotton division.

Jamsetji wanted his son Dorab to meet the high scholar and respected Dr. H.J. Bhabha, who lived with his daughter Meherbai. When he got there, he also met Bhabha's daughter Meher. This meeting later ended in their marriage. At the time of this marriage in 1897, Dorabji was 38 years old, while Meherbai was only 18 years old.

Dorabji had all the qualities of the Tata family for which they were well-known. These qualities are — initiative, resourcefulness, leadership and achievement of purpose. It was the result of his thinking and foresight that he fulfilled all his father's dreams, which Jamsetji could not realize during his life. With the help of his close relative R.D. Tata, he first focused on the projects his father had started. The first of these was the establishment of a modern iron and steel industry — the result of which is Tata Steel.

Along with that, with his increased morale he set up 'Tata Power' to supply electricity to the industries. These two are integral parts of the 'Tata Industry Group' today.

He served as a driving force for each member of his team. Whatever project he took up, he was completely attached to it. He kept a close watch on every detail and even travelled to mineral fields with scientists and explorers engaged in the discovery of cast iron.

The Tata group expanded significantly under the leadership of Dorabji. It expanded rapidly and diversified beyond Jamsetji's era to just three textile factories and the Taj Hotel. In addition to the largest steel company in the personal sector it soon managed and owned an integrated steel plant, three hydroelectric power companies, a large edible oil and soap factory and two cement factories. Apart from these, the Indian Institute of Science, Bangalore was established during the tenure of Dorabji. In 1910, the King of England conferred him with the title of Knighthood (Sir). In this way he was appreciated and honoured for his works.

Dorabji had an abiding interest in sports. This attachment towards sports was further enhanced when he studied at Cambridge. In order to increase interest and improve the level of sports in India, he started the 'Olympic Movement'. As the President of the Indian Olympic Association in 1924, he bore the expenses of the Indian batch participating in the Paris Olympics. He was also elected a member of the International Olympic Association.

❑

Lady Meherbai

Dorabji's wife Meherbai has a remarkable place in India's women's movement. She was always devoted to the education and the welfare of Indian women. She was the founding member of the 'Bombay Presidency Women's Council' and later the 'National Council of Women'. She agitated movements for giving higher education to women, abolition of purdah and eradication of untouchability. In this work she was fully supported by Dorabji. She called a surveyor from England to conduct a survey of girls' education in India. The survey was continued for one year and came out in the form of a book, which served as a pioneer for women's education for the next several years.

Her speech about India and Indians at the Bottle Creek College, America was compendious, covering every aspect of Indian life and society. Like Dorabji, she too was very fond of sports. She was a good tennis player and won many awards as well. Together they participated in many All India Championships and achieved success.

She was also an active member of the Indian Red Cross. During the war, she worked hard to raise donations. In recognition of her contribution, King George V honoured her himself.

She died of leukemia on June 18, 1931. Dorabji established the 'Lady Tata Memorial Trust' in 1932 in her memory. This trust was formed to study various blood-related diseases. In 1932, he established a trust fund, which was to be used for further work in research, disaster relief and other humanitarian purposes. The trust was named 'Sir Dorabji Tata Trust' and it is believed that he invested all his assets in this trust.

Dorabji also contributed significantly to the field of education. He gave an appreciable amount of money to Cambridge University for laboratory equipment. He also helped the 'Bhandarkar Oriental Research Institute' (Pune) financially to study Sanskrit.

He died on June 3, 1932 in Germany. His mausoleum remains near the tomb of his wife Meherbai in Brookwood Cemetery, England.

❑

Ratan Dadabhai Tata

Ratan Dadabhai Tata renowned as R.D. Tata was born in Navsari in 1856. It was here that he got his primary education. Later he received his higher education at Elphinstone College and then studied agricultural science in Madras.

After completing his education, he started his work with his father's company Tata & Co. When he began his work, the company's condition was not stable, the business was heading towards recession. Hence, he was sent to Hong Kong for company work.

Even after his father's death in 1876, he continued to work. In 1883, he took over the charge of the company. The company was not in an acceptable state at that time. This was the time when he got an opportunity to demonstrate his financial ability and got his company out of many problems and vicious circles.

Jamsetji was very impressed with the calibre of R.D. Tata. Therefore, in 1884, he made him a part of his company 'Empress Mills'. After this, in 1887, he was incorporated as a partner in his newly formed company, 'Tata and Sons.'

Ratan Dadabhai was associated with its manager Bejanji Dadabhai Mehta in the 'Empress Mills'. Bejanji was then looking after the technical and management work, while Ratan Dadabhai was entrusted with the financial side. During the same period, he was entrusted with the task of opening a factory in Yavatmal along with his cousin, Dorabji Tata. The economic condition of the indigenous mill was not satisfactory at that time, hence its financial workload was assigned to R.D. Tata. Together with Dorabji under the guidance of Jamsetji, he successfully carried out his work and helped the company to overcome difficulties.

The business of the company set up by Jamsetdji was different from that of Nausherwanji, so he gave the charge of the eastern branch to his cousin R.D. Tata. R.D. Tata moved to Hong Kong for a few years, where he set up branches in places like Shanghai, which ran the rice and silk business. This business flourished so much under his control that soon new branches opened in New York and Paris, which mainly traded in pearls and silk. It was in Paris that he fell in love with Suzanne Briere and in 1902 he married her.

After the death of Jamsetji, in 1907, the name of 'Tata and Sons' was changed to 'Tata Sons and Company'. It had three partners — Sir Dorabji, Sir Ratan Tata and R.D. Tata. The company operating from Hong Kong under the name of Tata & Co. was also merged with this new company.

R. D. Tata's main concern was to look after business and financial work while staying in the Bombay headquarters. While staying here he played a pivotal role in completing the projects — Iron and Steel Company, Hydroelectric Company and Indian Institute of Science, envisaged by Jamsetji. After the death of Sir Ratan Tata in 1918, R.D. Tata took over the important departments of the company. During the First World War when the company was going through a period of hardship, it was the work efficiency of R.D.Tata that helped the company overcome such a difficult period. This was possible only because of his mature experience and unparalleled guidance.

Despite serious economic difficulties, he was always devoted to welfare works and humanity.

He was also a member of the 'Imperial Legislative Council' for some time which later helped him in assuring the rescue of the iron and steel industry.

His visit to Japan in 1890 helped to develop the India-Japan trade relationship. The Japanese emperor recognized his work and conferred him with the title 'Third Order of the Rising Sun'. He died on August 26, 1926.

❑

Sir Ratan Tata

Jamsetji's younger son Sir Ratan Tata was born on January 20, 1871. He was 12 years younger than his brother Dorabji. He completed his education from St. Xavier's College, Bombay and married Nawazbai in 1892.

After marriage, Ratan lived in Esplanade House with his parents and wife. After the death of his father Jamsetji, he made Brightland his place of residence in the Marine Line. He later built a magnificent building for himself on Wodby Road, which was completed in 1915. He was able to stay in this building only for a few months, after which he went to England for his treatment and then died there.

After the death of his father Jamsetji, started working in a French insurance company, whose agent in India was 'Tata and Sons'. He also handled the work of 'Tata and Company', which did business of textiles, yarn, silk, pearls and rice. It had branches in Paris, Shanghai, Kobe, New York and Rangoon.

Although Sir Ratan Tata was associated with the functioning of 'Tata and Sons', most of its responsibility was assumed by his elder brother Dorabji. Ratan took a special interest in land acquisition in Mahim and Bandra and later the government undertook this task.

Sir Ratan Tata was socially very active. He had a keen interest in travelling as well. In the latter part of his life, every year he used to spent much of his stay in England. He was a member of the 'Carlton Club', London and was considered a respected member of the High Society of England. In 1906, he bought 'York House' in Twickenham, near London, England, and developed a beautiful garden in an area of 12 acres adjacent to it.

Social consciousness was one his qualities. He was fully aware of the importance of the struggle made under the leadership of Mahatma Gandhi against the excesses of the British in South Africa. Therefore, he not only gave it moral support but helped in financial terms as well. As a contribution to this struggle, he sent ₹ 1,25,000 to Gandhiji in five instalments. On the other hand, he gave adequate support and cooperation to the excellent work being done by Gopal Krishna Gokhale and his 'Servants of India Society' in the country. He also gave a total financial assistance of ₹ 1,10,000 to this movement under his generous support.

Sir Ratan was very agitated after seeing the poverty and plight of India and its people and he wanted to improve it. He urged that this matter should be investigated in a scientific manner. In 1912, he proposed financial assistance to the University of London to set up a body to work in this direction, so that suggestions could be made for identifying and diagnosing the causes of poverty and poor conditions. It was formed in 1913 and Sir Ratan accepted to give aid for three years at the rate of 1,400 pounds per year. In 1916, it was extended for five years. Even after his death this payment was made by his trustees till 1931. Many candidates did their research in this area and presented papers as well.

Sir Ratan Tata also provided economic assistance to the 'London School of Economics' to open its department for the study of 'Social Sciences'. This new department was called 'Ratan Tata Department of Social Sciences' in 1919. Later the 'London School of Economics' took its complete charge and accordingly its name was also changed.

Sir Ratan Tata was also very interested in India's past. In 1912, he proposed to provide economic assistance for archaeological survey and excavation in Bihar and Odisha. Accordingly, extensive excavation in Pataliputra, was done under the supervision of Dr. A.B. Spooner. From 1913 to 1917, Sir Ratan Tata provided assistance of ₹ 75,000 for this work. Many coins, terracotta items and other valuable materials were found in this excavation, which are still preserved in the Patna Museum.

Sir Ratan Tata was very kind-hearted and magnanimous. He gave donations for any such work, which affected him and contributed greatly for relief in the event of natural calamities like floods, famines or earthquakes. Apart from this, he also provided financial assistance to public monuments, schools and hospitals. He financed ₹ 10,000 per year for ten years to the 'George V Anti-Tuberculosis League'. The institute operated by this institution used to treat poor patients of tuberculosis. In 1916, he was awarded the title of Knighthood (Sir) for his various service works.

He was also an ardent admirer of art. During his travels both at home and abroad, he collected photographs, oil paintings, guns, swords, silverware, manuscripts, characters and carpets, which were important in terms of art and education. Later he handed over the collection to the Prince of Wales Museum, Bombay.

In 1916, Sir Ratan visited China and Japan. He fell ill after his return. The doctors advised him to go to England for treatment. He left for England in October 1916 with his wife Nawazbai and Secretary P.P. Mistry. On the way, their ship fell victim to the torpedoes of the Germans. Although Ratanji was rescued along with all the other passengers, this delay on the way had an adverse effect on his health.

He died in September 1918 in St Abbs, Carnival. His mausoleum is in Brookwood Cemetery, London near his father's mausoleum.

Sir Ratan Tata had no child on heir. In his will, he devoted a considerable part of his wealth to philanthropic works.

❑❑

Lady Nawazbai

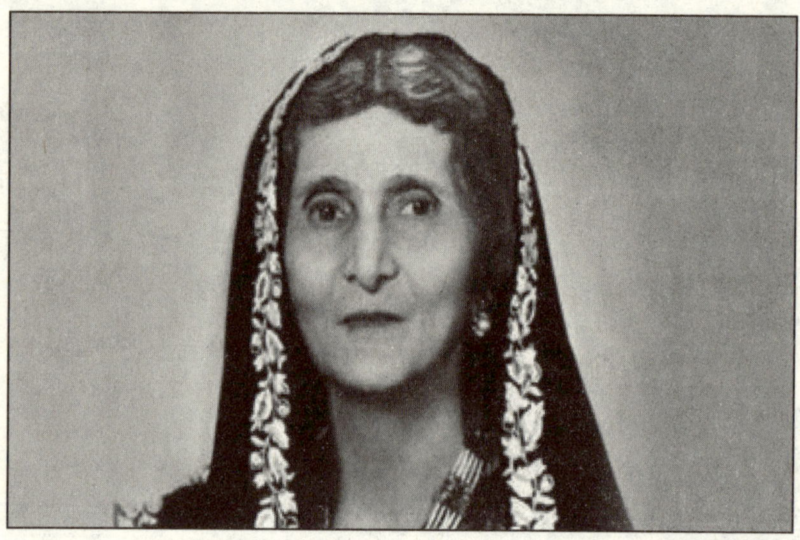

Nawazbai, the wife of Sir Ratan, was born in September 1877. She was married to Sir Ratan in 1890 and was proficient in horse riding and polo. They had spent a part of their lives in London and the couple was highly respected among the elite. Like Sir Ratan Tata, Lady Nawazbai was also a great admirer of fine art. Her contribution to the collection of various artifacts cannot be underestimated.Nawazbai was widowed at the age of 41. She had a great responsibility to take care of the estate of Sir Ratan and spent the rest of her life in a dignified way in the 'Tata House'.

After the untimely death of Sir Ratan, Nawazbai was inducted into the governing board of 'Tata Sons' in 1918. She held this position till her death. She died in August 1965.

She was the first and only woman to be a member of the governing board of 'Tata Sons'. A generous donation to the 'National Metallurgical Research Institute' in Jamshedpur exemplifies her immense and generous heart. By this, she demonstrated her willingness to spend the fund of Sir Ratan Tata Trust in creative work.

In 1928, she played a major and key role in the establishment of the 'Ratan Tata Institute'. Through this, instead of giving cash assistance to the people, it worked towards providing necessary training and employment opportunities to the poor and needy people in individual institutions. She worked for the welfare of everyone and was above the spirit of religion, sect and caste.

As Chairperson of the 'Sir Ratan Tata Trust', she invited S.J.I. Markham of the Carnage Trust to study the problems of the Parsi community and present a report on it. With this move, Parsi Charities organized themselves to make their 'charity' capable.

Childless Nawazbai wished for the survival of her husband's legacy, so she adopted Naval Hormusji Tata, son of Hormusji Tata. In this way, this adopted son of Lady Nawazbai later took over the work of the Tata family.

❑❑

Naval Hormusji Tata

Naval Hormusji Tata was born on August 30, 1904 in Bombay to a middle-class family.

His father Hormusji Tata was a spinning master in a mill in Ahmedabad. His father died when he was just four years old. This was a great shock to his family. It was a difficult task for their widowed mother to raise her growing children. His relatives in Bombay brought them some relief. After that, their family house in Navsari became their shelter and refuge.

Eventually the family settled in Surat. Their necessary expenses were met from the income of zardozi work being done by their mother.

Meanwhile, Dorabji arrived on the scene. With his help, two of Naval's brothers got shelter in the J.N. Petit Parsi orphanage. There were about 300 children in this orphanage, for whom a limited amount of money was available in the form of budget for food, clothes and health. It was more or less a difficult life.

Staying in this position, this child later went on to reach a prominent position at the Tata Institute. It was a unique blend of his determination and personal qualities that brought him to this milestone of success.

As it is well known that Jamsetji Tata was married to Heerabai. He had two sons — Dorabji and Ratanji, who had no heir. When he was growing up in an orphanage, he was adopted by Sir Ratan Tata's wife, Lady Nawazbai.

Sir Ratan Tata died in England in 1918 at the age of 47. At a meeting of family members chaired by Sir Dorabji, it was decided that a son was a must for 'Utthama Sanskar', so one should be adopted as a son. Naval's mother was Sir Ratan's favourite cousin, so it was decided to adopt Naval. Nawazbai accepted this family decision and thus Naval Hormusji Tata was adopted. Nawazbai immediately wanted to take Naval out of the orphanage, but the rules of the orphanage came in the way. He was able to leave from there only when he passed his tenth examination while living there.

Although he suddenly became a member of an influential family in the country, but he never forgot his past. He used to say that "I am thankful to God, who gave me the opportunity to experience the sufferings of poverty, which moulded my personality accordingly in the years to come."

After completing his Bachelor's in Economics from Bombay University, he went to England to complete a short course in accountancy. After returning from there in 1930, he entered the Tata organization as Dispatch Clerk Assistant Secretary.

He soon joined the post of Assistant Secretary at Tata Sons. In 1933, he was made Secretary in the Department of Aeronautics and was later transferred to the textile department as an executive. Seeing his abilities, he was made Joint Managing Director of the textile factories operated by Tata in 1939. In 1941, he was promoted as a director in Tata Sons. In 1948, he took over as the managing director of Tata Oil Mills Company Limited. Prior to this, he had already become the chairman of Tata Mills. In the following years he was promoted swiftly. He was made the chairman of other textile factories and three electric companies and later was appointed vice-president at Tata Sons.

In this way, he had the direct responsibility of managing four textile mills, three power companies and the Sir Ratan Tata Trust. Apart from this, he was also responsible for guiding several other companies and trusts of the group.

Despite being surrounded by work engagements, he maintained his calm nature, goodwill and humility like qualities in his personality and never forgot his past.

Despite his busy schedule at Bombay House, he used to meet people of all sections of society. He was very fond of various trusts operated under the name Tata; because the work of these trusts was based on a spirit of philanthropy. Therefore, he felt a personal liability towards these works.

He was the President of the Indian Cancer Society for nearly 30 years and also contributed appreciably to the field of sports. He was the President of the 'Indian Hockey Federation' from 1946 to 1961, was the first chairman of the 'All India Council for Sports' and also provided services to the 'International Hockey Federation'.

Despite a tiring lifestyle during the day, he kept himself fresh and was humorous as well. He was a very social and simple man. The employees also enjoyed his interesting jokes and respected him.

Naval's work on labour relations was also much better than his predecessors. He was an honest and open person and had a keen interest in solving the problems of the working class. According to the situations, he expressed his views and considered all options adequately to solve a problem.

In 1946, he represented the Indian textile industry in the International Labour Union. His ideas were highly appreciated. In 1957, he was elected a member of the Regulatory Committee of the International Trade Union and remained its member until his death in 1989. In 1966, he was elected as a member of the 'Labour Panel' of the Planning Commission in the country.

'The National Institute of Labour Management' was established by him, which is today known as the 'National Institute of Personal Management'. He was also its president from 1951 to 1980. He worked to bridge the growing gap between the owners and employees due to various reasons. He suggested fair and appropriate measures and considered himself an advocate of employee interests and did continuous and remarkable work for their rights and interests. He also took full care of the interests of the employees of the unorganized sector.

He was the President of the Indian Hockey Federation for many years. During his presidential tenure, India won three consecutive Olympic gold medals in Olympic hockey. Tata Sports Club played a seminal role in serving Indian hockey.

He was rich in an all-round versatile talent. Many times, he offered his services to several institutions simultaneously, such as the Indian Institute of Science, Swadeshi League, Bombay State Social Welfare Council, National Safety Council etc. He was also the chairman of several public welfare trusts.

On Republic Day in 1969, the President honoured him with the 'Padma Vibhushan'. In the same year he was honoured for his contribution to maintaining industrial peace.

Naval Hormusji Tata was married to Sunu but his household life was not pleasant. After the divorce of Naval and Sunu, Lady Nawazbai took over the responsibility of raising their sons, Ratan and Jimmy.

On May 5, 1989, Naval Hormusji died of a simple heart and reformative tendency. He was in favour of giving everyone equal opportunities for progress.

❑❑

J.R.D. Tata

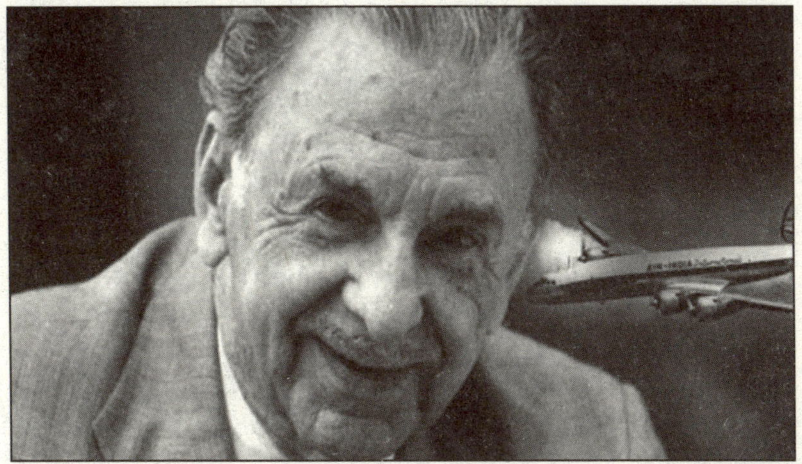

Jahangir Ratan Dadabhai (J.R.D.) was born on July 29, 1904 in Paris. His mother was French. His father's name was Ratan Dadabhai Tata. He was known among people as Jamsetji's cousin and R.D. Educated in France, Japan and other countries, he also served primary service in the French army for one year. He wished to remain in the army, but fate had planned something else for him. So he had to say goodbye to the French army. He wanted to pursue engineering education from Cambridge University, but in the meantime, he received a message from his father to return to India and complied as an obedient son. Returning here, he found himself in an environment and business empire that he was not used to. His work started as an assistant at Tata Sons. Shortly after his father's death he was inducted as a director in the company in 1926. He was appointed chairman in 1938. J.R.D. was a charismatic person.

He contributed to the industrial development of India for almost 53 years. On March 25, 1991, he handed over the charge of Tata Sons to his junior partner Ratan Naval Tata. The board of Tata Sons unanimously elected him as its lifetime chairman (retired).

J.R.D. is considered the founder of civil aviation in India. He was the first pilot in India to achieve this qualification. In 1932, he founded India's first national carrier, Tata Airlines. In 1946, it was renamed as 'Air India Limited'. The inaugural flight of Tata Airlines travelled between Karachi to Bombay and was operated by J.R.D. himself. In the following years, he established Air India International Ltd. as a joint venture with the Government of India for long-haul international flights. He was its executive chairman till its nationalization in 1953.

On his suggestion, the Government of India set up two flying corporations—Air India and Indian Airlines, which were formed for international and domestic flights respectively. He was appointed the chairman of Air India and continued working in this post till 1978.

At the age of 78, on the fiftieth anniversary of Indian Civil Aviation, he repeated his 1932 inaugural flight in a 50-year-old aircraft on October 15, 1982.

He was awarded several awards for his contribution to the aeronautical field. In 1948, he was awarded the rank of Honorary Group Captain in the Indian Air Force and in 1966 as Air Commodore (Honorary). Apart from this, he also received many international awards.

He cared for Tata Airlines like a child. He had worked hard in its imagery, from the outline to putting it on the practical plane and later in its development and care. This was the reason that he strongly opposed the nationalization of Air India by Jawaharlal Nehru in 1953. Nehru gave him the leeway to take control and management of the cargo planes, from where he was separated in 1977 by a law.

Operations of Air India were an example of J.R.D.'s excellent efficiency. The principles of socialism were then highly prevalent. Industries had to work under various rules and restrictions, yet J.R.D. tried his best to lead the country on the path of industrial upliftment.

It is also clear from this that when J.R.D. took over the position of chairman of Tata Sons, then the Tata group had 14 companies under its control. In his nearly 50-year tenure, that is, until July 1988, there were 95 companies that were started or controlled by the Tata group. Under his mature leadership, the Tata group expanded in all directions. Prominent among them are electricity, engineering, hotels, consultancy services, information technology, consumer goods and other industrial products.

His contribution in the field of science and medicine is also unique. During his tenure, Tata Institute of Social Science, Tata Institute of Fundamental Research, National Institute of Advanced Sciences, and Tata Memorial Hospital touched amazing heights in their respective fields.

J.R.D. gave a new direction to the current business practices at that time. Instead of adopting the practice of running an enterprise under the supervision of members of the households, they adopted a purely commercial approach. Bringing the talent forward, harnessing their skills and giving them an opportunity to grow. Some difficulties and obstacles also came his way, but he faced those challenges.

For J.R.D., the aim of national interest lay in the progress of the country and he made his full contribution in this direction. The idea of donating at the simple level and having a sense of fulfilment of his duty was not acceptable to him, rather, he gave priority to such works which were sustainable and gave permanent results. Keeping this in mind, the multi-purpose 'Tata Trust' was established in 1944. J.R.D. established the 'Thelma Tata Trust' in Bombay with the proceeds from the sale of his shares. The aim of this trust was to improve the status of women from disadvantaged sections and to lead them towards progress.

He was an advocate of family planning and population control in the interest of the country. In recognition of his efforts, he was awarded the UN Population Award in September 1992 and was the founding member of the 'Family Planning Institute'. He was also the Chairman of the Governing Body of the Tata Institute of Fundamental Research, Member of the Atomic Energy Commission and President of the Court of the Indian Institute of Science, Bangalore. He served as chairman of the 'J.N. Tata Endowment for the Higher Education of Indians' and 'Homi Bhabha Fellowship Council.' Along with this, he handled the post of chairman of the Sir Dorabji Tata Trust, J.RD. Tata Trust and Jamsetji Trust.

He also received many national and international awards. Prominent among them were 'Padma Vibhushan', 'Legion of Honour' of France, 'Order of Merit of the Federal Republic of Germany' and doctoral degrees from Allahabad, Bombay, Roorkee and Banaras University. The Government of India honoured him with the 'Bharat Ratna', the highest civilian honour of the country in 1992. He died in Geneva in November 1993.

J.R.D. had met Thelma in France. His romance with Thelma resulted in a happy marriage and they got married in 1930. He was childless, but he accepted it as God's will. Although, he is not among us but his legacy will always remain alive. The country will always remember him.

❑

Ratan Tata

Ratan Naval Tata was born in 1937 in Bombay in the rich and famous Tata family. He is the son of Sunu and Naval Hormusji Tata.

Ratan's childhood was unfortunate as well. When he was just seven years old, his parents got divorced. Ratan and his brother Jimmy were raised by their grandmother Nawazbai. She had great affection for Ratan. Ratan Tata did his early education at Campion School in Bombay. At the age of fifteen, he was sent to the United States to pursue further studies. He received his bachelor's degree in Architecture and Structural Engineering in 1962 from Cornell University, USA. He also did a course in the Advanced Management Programme from the Harvard Business School.

After returning to India in 1962, he entered the Tata group. At that time, J.R.D. was the chairman of the Tata group. He sent Ratan to Jamshedpur to work at Tata Steel, so that he could understand the work of Tata Steel properly. There he worked like the other employees only, wearing a blue uniform. It included all the work from removing the limestones with shovels to work related to the blazing furnaces.

In 1971, he was given charge of the National Radio and Electronics Company (NELCO). NELCO was going through economic difficulties at that time. Nobody expected its success. But looking at the future of Tata Company, Ratan succeeded in convincing the then chairman J.R.D. that more investment was needed in the company. Although, J.R.D. was not keen to invest more in it.

This was the time when the country was under the dominating influence of license and permit. As a result, he had to face many difficulties in carrying out his work. These difficulties gave him a new vision. Therefore, he focused on improving his abilities and in 1975 received higher education in management from the Harvard School. In December 1988, he was made the chairman of Telco. After the death of his father in 1989, he took over the charge of Sir Ratan Tata Trust as chairman.

During his tenure, J.R.D. Tata broadened the basis of Tata Sons. As a result, in 1980 where there were only 11 directors, by 1991 their number increased to 18. It included those people who played a key role in the development of the Tata Group. In later years, this kept changing.

On March 25, 1991, J.R.D. Tata proposed Ratan Naval Tata for the post of Chairman of Tata Sons as his successor and retired on his own.

❑❑

Tata Group's Journey Under the Leadership of Ratan Tata

When Ratan Tata took over the charge of the 104-year-old Tata Group, his predecessor, J.R.D. Tata had handled this work for almost 50 years. He gave the group a new shine, while on the other hand he also left an impression of his personal style. In the latter half of J.R.D.'s tenure, the powerful chairman and managing directors of various Tata Group institutions, which were closely associated with J.R.D., tried to leave their mark and imprint on the companies related to them in the backdrop of the closeness of their relationship.

In July 1991, the central government abolished many provisions of the M.R.T.P. and moved towards liberalization. This task of the government was quite a relief for Ratan Tata, who took charge three months after.

When Ratan Tata rose to the position of chairman, the operations of individual companies were in the hands of powerful chairmen or managing directors and they operated in their own way. The main challenge for him was to bring them all together. He set the age of retirement for the post of chairman and managing director. This age was 75 years for the chairman and 65 years for the managing director. He organized the erstwhile companies, made sure to come out of some others, set up new companies and later acquired some. He made 32 new starts in the first decade of his tenure.

It was clear till the death of J.R.D. (1993), that Ratan Tata's attempt to organize the group companies under the banner of 'Tata Sons', had the blessing of J.R.D. with him. In this period of liberalization, the 'Tata' holding company gradually increased its share ratios in group companies such as Tisco (Tata Steel), Tata Chemicals, Telco (Tata Motors) and Tata Tea. Under him, Tata Consultancy Services was publicized. Meanwhile, Tata Motors was listed on the New York Stock Exchange.

In order to facilitate the operations, the Tata group sold its shares in the last decade of the century in a number of sectors such as edible oils (TOMCO), cosmetics (Lakme), pharmaceuticals (Rallis & Merind), paints (Goodlass Nerolac). In addition, he sold assets in ACC, computer and telecommunication hardware and oil. They split from joint ventures like IBM Timex.

Between 1990 and 2002, his main focus was on cars, telecom, insurance and fertilizers. Today, in the twenty-first century Tata Group's scope of work can be mainly divided into the following seven areas-

(a) **Materials:** Such as steel and advanced plastics

(b) **Chemicals:** Inorganic fertilizers, pesticides

(c) **Engineering:** Automobiles, auto components, air conditioning

(d) **Energy:** Energy

(e) **Consumer goods:** Tea, coffee, watches

(f) **Services:** Hotel, retail, finance services, insurance, international trade

(g) **Information methods:** Software, industrial & telecom, automation & telecom

As soon as Ratan Tata took over as the chairman, he laid the foundation stone for many technology businesses and aimed at the development of numerous ventures. Under the efficient direction of J.R.D., he started giving form to his imagination and creativity related to the Tata group. It was a transition period. With the beginning of liberalization, new beliefs and rules were replacing old beliefs and systems.

With the change in the central industrial policy, the government was also trying to remove all the discrepancies in the establishment of individual undertakings and to create a suitable environment for their development to an extent. As a result, some public sector domains were opened up to the private sector. The economy that was confined and shrunk under the cloak of socialism for around a decade got the chance to spread. The economic policies of some countries had changed and this phase continued in many countries. In such a situation, the Government of India also understood that liberal policies are needed to achieve good economic growth.

Ratan Tata also benefited from this new thinking and situation. As a result, he made strides in many new areas of the industry. It is also worth mentioning here that the Tata Group's overseas emoluments grew significantly due to the 'Tata Consultancy Service'. It was established by Ratan Tata only in the 80s. Soon it became an acclaimed name in the consultancy sector on the world stage.

❑❑

Ratan Tata's Foresight

When Ratan Tata took over the command of Tata Sons, not only the Tata Group but the entire country witnessed a change in the old trends. With the liberalization of the Indian economy and change in the thinking of the global economy a new era of opportunities and challenges was unfolded. He took many steps to meet these challenges and to convert the available opportunities into success.

To increase holdings in companies managed by Tata: With this thought, by 2002 the holding in Tata Steel increased from 8 to 26 per cent, in Telco from 17 to 32 per cent, in Voltas from 22 to 25 per cent. In some other companies like Tata Chemicals, Tata Tea etc. it remained unchanged (30 per cent). In some new companies the holdings were 76 per cent in Tata Infotech, 26 percent in Trent Ltd. and 50 per cent in Infomedia.

A Group Executive Office was established in 1998 as a part of the operation and consolidation of the Group's policies. In this a group chairman and 5 members, who were from group company, group finance, group human resources and new group project were included.

Later in 2002, Tata Group Corporate Centre was set up, with Group Executive Officers as members. It included — Ratan Tata, Dr. J.J. Irani, R.K. Krishnakumar, M.A. Sunawala, R. Gopalakrishnan, Ishat Hussain and K.A. Chokar.

A code of conduct was prepared to use the name 'Tata'. If anyone disregarded it, he had to stop using the name 'Tata'. The Tata model of business excellence was launched in 1994.

Seeing the importance of the Tata brand, the Tata companies were expected to work for the further development of the brand name.

When Ratan Tata took over, his main challenge at that time was to bring companies under one framework so that they could work in one direction. He tightened his grip on companies. Although, to a larger extent the autonomy of the company was with him only, but he retained the right to submit his objection in the event of disagreement as a shareholder in major policy decisions and to bring it to a definite outcome.

Today, the Tata Group is not a loose association of different companies, but a closely connected group, which is headed in the direction to meet the challenges of the future.

❑

Strong Intention

Tata Chemicals and Telco were counted as two of the largest companies in India till 1980, but an untoward occurred with Telco in 2000-01. Overnight, the market for its products fell by 45 per cent and the company incurred a loss of ₹ 500 crore. In fact, from 1993 to 1997, Telco sales had increased by ₹ 7,500 crore. The sales fell flat when ₹ 1,700 crore was spent on the company's Indica car project. In such a situation, a huge reduction in sales and loss of ₹ 500 crore was a major challenge for the company and its employees. It was a direct injury to the self-respect of the employees and officers. They unanimously decided that the situation had to be overcome. The fact was that only the employees and officers of the company could handle this situation well, because they knew where and what the problem was and what was the solution.

Ratan Tata, linked this sense of self-esteem of the employees successfully to the company's resurgence and made successful use of it. And in the third financial year itself, i.e. in the year 2002-03, the company reached a profit of ₹ 500 crore (pre-condition). This achievement was nothing short of a miracle under the erstwhile circumstances.

He gave a new edge to the company in the difficult problematic situation. A task force was formed at a higher level. In no time, forty action teams were formed, with 230 operation managers working on the allocated work. All these teams were from Tata Motors and Consultant sources. These teams worked day and night, made the data available to the concerned departments and after that the suitability was examined from the operational point of view. The deficiencies were determined and work started accordingly.

The senior manager team met many young employees and high-level executors from the chairman to the senior officials and got their views, took suggestions from them about the problems and appropriate steps were taken accordingly.

The second task was the use of special training programmes and inspirational steps. For this, mixed groups of employees of all grades and management personnel of all levels were sent to workshops for training and motivation. The focus of higher leadership was to create a result-oriented work culture devoid of all kinds of shortages. It was this work culture that made impossible goals possible.

Tata Indica has been Ratan Tata's dream since 1993, which was realized in 1999. Telco officials toured around the world to fulfil this dream. Actually, he wanted a car that suited the Indian situation. It should have the same space like the Ambassador, Zen-like exterior design, Italian style and the French engine design. Ratan Tata had a mental connect with this project. So when he accepted the challenge, he worked hard for the success in that proportion only. When it became necessary, he received expertise from all the possible sources, but developed it on its own. Hence, it was truly a national achievement.

As a result, when Indica came out of the showroom in 1999, the company had 1,15,000 bookings in which the entire amount was paid in advance. From this only its fame can be guessed. Later on, many improvements were made and many other models like Indica V2, Indigo, Indica Sedan etc. were developed.

Rovers in England needed a world class car in the same segment. Hence, it tied up with Telco to sell the Indica V2 in England and the European continent, and in five years a total of 100,000 cars were to be sold as City Rover. Its first batch was sent in 2003.

Tata Chemical was a leading company in its field in India's pre-liberalization era. In 1990 it made three new beginnings. They were — Babrala Fertilizer Plant in Uttar Pradesh, the establishment of Tata Kisan Kendra and production of branded edible salt. Out of these, the Babrala plant was started in 1994. Urea was to be produced in it. Along with this, an ammonia plant was also established in the same complex. Babrala Complex had set new records in the fields of production, technology, energy conservation and safety.

Despite this, in the year 1999, an odd situation arose owing to the heavy arrival of soda ash from China and reduction in the fixed rate of urea. For the first time in the company's history, it had to declare a loss for the quarter that ended in June 2000.

As a result, a new management committee was formed. Working under Prasad Menon, the committee had to earn the company from afresh by refocusing the factors responsible for the company's position. It took some important steps of a different nature. These steps had the desired effect and in 2001-02 the amount of profit reached ₹ 200 crore.

It was Ratan Tata's foresight that helped to take all the necessary steps to deal with an imminent threat, and Tata Chemicals not only returned to its track but also started to gallop.

Tata Steel was in strict need of renewal to remain in competition during the period of liberalization and this renovation required retrenchment of about 35,000 employees. At that time, both the factories and mines of Tata Steel had a total of 78,000 employees. Everyone was aware of its immediate consequences of sorting on such a large scale, but sorting was equally necessary. After the estimation of profit and loss was made under Ratan Tata's leadership, it was concluded that this problem could be solved easily if some attractive conditions were laid down for retrenchment of employees. The adverse effects from these conditions would be eliminated within a few years of modernization and eventually it was a profitable deal. The conditions for voluntary leave were so attractive that several employees applied for voluntary leave and soon the company got rid of the additional employees. All this was achieved by maintaining great ease and industrial harmony. This is the reason why Tata Steel not only remained in competition in the coming years but also surpassed miles. Not only this, it was also able to acquire heavily competitive steel companies.

Ratan Tata's strong intentions are also reflected in the Singur land acquisition dispute case, where he preferred to move away instead of succumbing to some people's stubbornness.

❑

Some Famous Tata Owned Companies and Brands

Tata Group is India's largest business group in terms of market order and revenue. Established as a multinational company, the headquarters of this group is in Mumbai. It is recognized as a respected group all over the world. Its main areas of business are steel, automobiles, information technology, communication, energy, tea and hotels, etc. Its business is spread over 85 countries across 6 continents. Its products and services are exported to 80 countries of the world.

Engaged in 7 business sectors, this group is organized from 98 companies. Of these, 27 companies are listed as public companies and 65.8 per cent of the Tata Group is owned by its charitable trusts. The largest share in the group is of Tata Steel, Corus Steel, Tata Motors, Tata Communications, Tata Consultancy Services, Tata Power, Tata Tea, Titan Industries, Tata Teleservices and Taj Hotels.

❑

Tata Steel

Founded on the belief of Tata, Tata Steel is the first steel plant not only in India but also in Asia. Tata Steel has created a new history by acquiring the Anglo-Dutch steel company Corus. This is the largest acquisition by an Indian company abroad and is in keeping with Tata Steel's reputation.

Jamsetji struggled hard to establish a steel plant, but he died three years before the site was sought. Before his death, he ensured that his dream came true. Members of the team that fulfilled his dream were- his son Dorabji Tata, expert surveyor C.M. Weld and Shapurji Saklatwala and Charles Page Perrin, Consulting Engineers, and Jamsetji himself went to New York to invite them.

Perrin prepared a detailed project report of the company's plant. Even after submitting the report, Charles Perrin stayed in India till the decision to establish the plant at Sakchi was made. Sakchi's name was later changed to Jamshedpur and this conversion of name was done by Lord Chelmsford, the then Viceroy of India. Only then did the Kalimati station get the name 'Tata Nagar'.

In those days, the spirit of Swadeshi was in spate. Based on this sentiment, Tata Iron and Steel Company turned towards the Indian capital market and on August 26, 1907, issued shares for sale.

Investment letters were received from 8,000 Indian investors in just three weeks. The Maharaja of Gwalior purchased the entire 40,000-pound debenture issued for the availability of working capital. A sum of 2.32 crore was raised by issuing common, primary and deferred shares, through which a steel plant of 72,000 tonnes annual production capacity was to be set up. Installation of the plant started in 1908 and the first body was produced in February 1912. Tata had 11 per cent stake in this company.

More than once, it was threatened with its takeover by the government. To prevent this possibility, a bill was introduced in the Central Legislative Assembly in 1924. This idea was fuelled for the second time during the Janata Party rule (1977–79) in 1977 by the then Minister of Industry, but nothing happened.

Jamsetji dreamed of doing something by setting up Tata Steel. Tata Steel's dream was fulfilled by Dorabji and J.R.D. Tata. But J.R.D. Tata was the person who increased Tata's assets from 62 crore to 10,000 crore in 1990. J.R.D. had the natural talent of testing man and developing leadership. He went on to help an outstanding manager like Russi Mody to excel and later raised him to a prestigious position. Mody improved the marketing operations and formed the Export Cell. He founded the 'G Blast Furnace', which according to the 2004 national record was the largest 'blast furnace' of Tata Steel.

J.R.D. Tata's successor Ratan Tata took over the charge of the steel company from Russi Mody in 1992. The company's competition was mainly about prices due to the liberalized Indian economy. Therefore, Tata Steel was not in a pristine condition at that time. The McKinsey report in the late 1990s advised Tata Steel to opt out of the steel business. But the real scene proved to be an eye opener. Successional changes were made in the company. Through advanced and attractive schemes, the company got rid of the excess of employees and the number of employees decreased from 78,000 to 43,000. This goal was achieved without harming the industrial harmony. The company distanced itself from many non-core businesses. The main thrust was to maintain the quality of steel as well as cost reduction and to bring prices to competitive levels using advanced technology. Meanwhile, a cold rolling mill was established. In 2001, B. Muthuraman replaced J.J. Irani as Managing Director of the company. Despite steep fluctuations in steel prices in 2001-02, Tata Steel was among the five steel companies in the world that made a profit. In the subsequent years, significant success was recorded through branded products and retail.

The company made several acquisitions over the past few years. Among these, the acquisition of Corus Steel is a historic event.

The company, which was earlier ranked 56th in steel production, has become the sixth largest steel producer in the world on its 100th year, it also grew significantly in the following years.

❑

Tata Chemicals

Tata Chemicals was established in 1939. Its first consignment of imported turbo generators from a foreign manufacturer were ruined due to the ongoing Second World War and sank into the sea. After this, its next shipment somehow reached Bombay. But the company's early years were not propitious. The company had to face many difficulties from installation to production. Its most profitable business would have been the production of soda ash, but at that time only 6 companies of the world had the technology to produce it. But Tata Chemicals prepared its formula on its own. The second task was to produce at least 400 tonnes daily. Darbari Seth, a Chemical Engineer, laid the entire outline of the chemical plant in front of J.R.D. Agreeing with him J.R.D. handed over the responsibility of engineering, fabrication and installation of new machines at Mithapur to him.

Darbari Seth and his team completed the work of installation by working indefatigably and at the same time ensured that they all worked together. As soon as the plant was ready, the target of producing 400 tons per day was also handed over to the same team. Within the first fortnight, production from the plant reached 545 tonnes per day.

Today Tata Chemicals Ltd. is the second largest soda ash producer in the world. Other than India, its production units are in other countries like UK, Kenya and USA.

Apart from this, the company also produces sodium bicarbonate, sulphuric acid and sodium tripoli phosphate on a large scale. Apart from this, Tata Chemicals Ltd. (TCL) is the largest producer of urea and phosphate fertilizers in India. Not only this, it is also the largest producer of branded iodized salt in India.

In 2003, Tata Chemicals gained control of Hindustan Lever Chemicals, the leader in the phosphate category in West Bengal, Bihar and Jharkhand. The Hindustan Lever Chemicals factory is in Haldia and Tata Chemicals factories are in Mithapur (Gujarat) and Babrala (UP). A plant for its nitrogen fertilizer production in Babrala was also in progress. Tata Chemicals has introduced a number of branded productions over the years due to its large and diverse dealer network and has made appreciable inroads through farmer training programmes.

Tata Kisan Kendras have done revolutionary work in this direction. Tata Chemicals also exports 10-15 per cent of its products.

❑❑

Tata Motors

Tata Motors is the largest automobile company in India. According to estimates in 2007-08, its revenue was ₹ 35,651 crore. It ranks highest in India in production in each category of commercial vehicles. As far as passenger vehicles are concerned, it is counted among the top three manufacturers. The company ranks fourth in truck production and second in bus production. Thus, it is a well-known name in the field of automobiles worldwide.

Telco (currently Tata Motors) was founded in 1945 and started production of vehicles in 1954. Today more than 40 lakh Tata vehicles are running on the roads of India and they have entered every corner of the country. Tata Motors' manufacturing units are located in Jamshedpur, Pune, Lucknow and Pantnagar (Uttarakhand).

In 1998, after many years of hard work and research, Ratan Tata launched the first Indian car known as Indica. Cars under its brand are Indigo and several other names were subsequently produced and exported to many countries. In 2004, Tata Motors acquired the Daewoo Commercial Vehicle Company of South Korea. It was the second largest truck manufacturer in South Korea. In this way, the restructured Tata Daewoo Commercial Vehicle Company launched several new vehicles in the Korean market and also started exporting them to other countries. In 2006, Tata Motors launched a mini truck in the market. It was quite successful and is in great demand in the market. As a result, its production has reached over 2,50,000 annually today.

In 2005, under a joint venture with Fiat, it has set up a new unit in Maharashtra to produce Fiat cars as well as Fiat powertrans and Tata cars.

The company is setting up new units at Dharwad in Karnataka and Sanand in Gujarat. The company has a network of around 3,500 centres for dealerships, sales and service and spare parts. It is also a distributor in the country of Fiat brand cars.

It also operates businesses in England, Thailand, South Korea and Spain through subsidiaries companies and ancillary units. These include the acquisition and operation of two well-known British brands Jaguar and Land Rover in 2008.

Earlier in 2006, Tata Motors formed a joint venture with Brazil's Marcopolo, which is world-renowned in the construction of buses and coaches, which will produce fully manufactured buses and coaches for export to the Indian market and other countries. In the same year the company became associated as a joint venture with the Thonburi Automotive Assembly Plant Company of Thailand, so that the company could produce and market the van for supply in Thailand. In 2008, the production of trucks called 'Xenon pickup trucks' had started at the Tata plant in Thailand.

The company had made a good place in the international market as well. The company's commercial and passenger vehicles are being marketed in many countries of Europe, Middle East Asia, South East Asia, South Asia, Africa and South America. Its joint ventures or franchises are working in Bangladesh, Ukraine, Kenya, Senegal and Russia.

The most important factor in the growth of the company in the last fifty years is - customer's need and satisfaction. For this there has been a tradition of research and development. About 2,500 scientists and engineers of the company's

Engineering Research Centre established in the year 1966, have made specific cooperation in the form of latest technologies and products for the use of the company. Apart from Pune, Jamshedpur, Lucknow in India, the research and development (R&D) centres of the company are working abroad in South Korea, Spain and England.

Tata Motors made the first light commercial vehicle in India and the indigenous passenger car Indica in 1998. It made significant inroads in the Indian market within its journey of only two years.

In January 2008, Tata Motors showcased the Nano, an affordable price car. This was in keeping with Ratan Tata's promise that he made with his countrymen promising an excellent low-cost car. It was named the 'people's car'. It was a laud effort for the world automobile industry. Nano is a car that fulfils the dream of a comfortable and safe journey for millions of families within their purchasing capacity. It is available in both standard and deluxe classes, in India. In the standard category, it has been priced at ₹ 1 lakh (excluding VAT and traffic expenses). That is why people have named it 'Lakhtakiya Car'.

This car has been built by assessing the needs of a common family. Accordingly, it has a relatively spacious passenger compartment, so that one can sit and spread one's legs easily. It is spacious enough for 4 passengers. It has an outstanding standard of regulatory safety standards required in India. Even in terms of pollution standards, it will emit much less pollution than all the two-wheelers being built in India. Keeping its weight light helped maximize performance by the energy consumed per unit. Due to high efficiency in energy consumption, the emission of carbon dioxide is also significantly reduced. Overall, this car is designed to be very useful for a small family.

Tata Motors can pave the way for an automobile revolution in the market by building many new advanced vehicles, in the coming years. All these vehicles will be technologically advanced and manufactured according to customer needs. These will use environment-friendly technologies and energy. The Research and Development department of Tata Motors strives for this overall.

Tata Motors is also engaged in engineering and automotive solutions through its ancillary units. Apart from this, it is also involved in manufacturing construction equipment, vehicle parts, machine tools and factory automation solutions, and manufacturing and service operation of automotive and computer applications parts.

Tata Motors is also conscious of its social commitments. It is a signatory to the United Nations' Global Compact and is engaged in community and labour-oriented social work in accordance with its principles.

Accordingly, it works in harmony with the welfare works and community development for the welfare of the rural population around its production units.

❑❑

Tata Tea

Tata Tea is the second largest tea company in the world, with a branded tea business spanning over 60 countries. The major companies in the Tata Tea Group are Tata Tea, the Tetley Tea Company of England acquired by Tata (this acquisition was made possible in 2004 at a cost of $ 407 million) and Tata Coffee.

The Tata Tea Group, established in 1964 as a joint venture with England's James & Finlay, is today trading in branded tea, coffee and other beverages. It also has its own tea gardens. While the Tata brand is at the top in India, the Tetley brand is the second largest 'tea bag' brand in the world. Apart from this, it also has its partnership in South Africa's 'Joekels Tea Packers' and the Polish tea brand 'Vitax and Flosana'.

Business Sector

Branded Tea- Tata Tea has five major brands in the country such as Tata Tea, Tetley, Chakra Gold, Kanan Devan and Gemini with access to all major segments of the consumer. Its distribution network extends to about 12 lakh retailers.

- **Instant Tea:** Tata Tetley's export unit exports several types of instant tea powder to the US.

- **Speciality Tea:** Tata Tea sells black, green and herbal teas under the brand names Tetley, Gemka and Good Earth.
- **Coffee:** Tata Coffee produces 9,000 tonnes of coffee annually. Tata's 'Eight O' Clock' coffee brand is the third largest coffee brand in America.
- **Tea gardens:** Tata Tea Company has around 50 tea gardens across India and also has a stake in certain plantations in Sri Lanka.

  Apart from these, the company also deals in energy drinks, 'Himalayan' brand mineral water. The joint ventures and ancillaries of Tata Tea are as follows-
- **Tata Coffee:** Formerly known as Consolidated Coffee, it is an ancillary unit of Tata Tea. Apart from this, Tata Tea also controls America's third largest coffee brand 'Eight O' Clock'.
- **Tata Tea:** The England-based Tetley Group's business spans the globe. It was acquired by Tata Tea in 2000.

Tata Tetley is an ancillary unit of Tata Tea, which deals with instant tea powder and exports it to the US.

Tata Tea Incorporation is a Florida-based ancillary unit of Tata Tea which supplies the bulk of instant tea powder to manufacturers.

Apart from this, Tata Tea is also associated with Mount Everest Mineral Water Company, which produces Himalayan brand mineral water. Tata Tea also has a stake in Sri Lanka's 'Watawala Plantations'.

Tata Tea produces and manufactures black tea through 18 tea gardens, in Kerala. This production and manufacturing is done through the 'Kanan Devan Hills Plantations Company'.

Recently, Tata Tea has entered into a joint venture agreement with China's 'Zhejiang Tea Import and Export Company' which will manufacture polyphenols and instant tea extracts.

Tata Power

'Tata Hydroelectric Power Supply Company' was established in 1911. The Andhra Valley Power Supply Company, established in 1916, was then integrated with it. Today, Tata Power Company Ltd. is India's largest private power generating company and has a power generation capacity of 2,300 Mega Watt. The idea of setting up some new units is underway and its production capacity is likely to increase significantly over the next few years. Tata Power works not only in the field of hydroelectricity, but also in solar and wind power generation. As a personal effort in the field of power generation in India, the first attempt was made by Tata Power in 1915 at Bhivpuri and Khopoli plants. The company's thermal power plants are operating at Trombay in Mumbai, Belgaum in Karnataka and Jojobera in Jharkhand. Hydroelectric power plants function in the Western Ghats and solar energy power plants in Ahmednagar.

The company is a pioneer in the introduction and operation of excellent energy technology. India's first 500 MW unit was set up at Trombay by Tata Power only. The company's line and distribution losses are the lowest at 2.4 per cent across India. For the last 90 years, Tata Power has provided excellent service to the power consumers in Bombay. A distribution unit of the company presently functions in Delhi as well. Established in a joint venture with the Delhi government, it is known as 'North Delhi Power Ltd.' (NDPL). This venture has been very successful. Initially, the agreement between the Delhi government and Tata Power was for 5 years, that was to be reviewed in 2005. According to the sources, it was later extended for the next 4 years. In these 5 years, the line and distribution losses of the related fields have come down from 51 per cent to 28 percent.

Tata Power Ltd. has implemented many projects in the Middle East, Africa and South East Asia. These include the installation of various Mega Watt projects in Dubai, Saudi Arabia, Kuwait, United Arab Emirates, Iran, etc.

Tata Power as a joint venture with Power Grid of India has agreed to partnership in the 1200 kilometre Taal Transmission Project. This is India's first transmission project which is based on government and private partnership.

Tata Power also obtained the contract to set up a 4,000 mega watt power plant at Mundra.

❑

Tata Consultancy Services

In the wake of the impending crisis of Monopoly Trade Restrictions (MRTP) in 1968, Tata Sons formed consultancy units on the basis of expertise. These were:

I. Tata Consultancy Services

II. Tata Consulting Engineers

III. Tata Economic Consultancy Services

IV. Tata Financial Services

After some initial strife Tata entrusted the responsibility to Faqir Chand, an outstanding electrical engineer, who was famous not only India but also in other countries due to his research papers and the discovery of excellent technology. For 1973-74 (two years) he was elected as one of the 30 members of the governing body of the American Institute that had membership of 3 lakh electric engineers. He also got an opportunity to visit many renowned institutions of America and inspect the research work going on there, as well as to know the views of his various colleagues.

He could well understand the upcoming information revolution and underlined India's bright future in the field of computers. He transformed Tata Consultancy Services (TCS) into a first level software engineering and service-provider. TCS was the one that developed the PAN (PAN) number for taxpayers for the Income Tax Department.

Today TCS has more than 1,12,000 IT consultants in about 50 countries of the world. Tata Consultancy Services is primarily in practice in the fields of IT services, business solutions and outsourcing.

Business Sector

Tata Consultancy Services has experience and expertise in many industries and service sectors. These include banking, financial services, health services, insurance, travel, traffic and hospitality services (hotels etc.), retail, energy, utilities, communication services, etc. It handles:

- **IT Services:** System Integration Solution, application development, testing solutions and management services.
- **Outsourcing:** Providing services and programmes that help in efficient work, business solutions and management of services.
- **Business solution:** Providing a strategy and solution that helps customers overcome their business-management challenge.
- **Advisory Services:** Setting business goals, designing strategies, implementing suggestions and assessing their effectiveness.
- **Engineering and Industrial Services:** Introducing solutions to companies in manufacturing sectors such as automotive, aerospace, industrial machinery, utility and pharmaceutical, etc., so that they can achieve engineering excellence and effective operations.
- **IT Infrastructure Services:** Providing services like- IT services, data centre management, End-user computing services, application management services, command centre services and management security services.

Apart from these, TCS also works in some other service sectors like business process outsourcing, enterprise solutions, full services, etc.

TCS is also involved in the field of innovation with full vigour. It has excellent laboratories for acquiring advanced technology, which are working to research and obtain new products in the new technology area. This includes new generation software processes, human-computer interfaces, nanotechnology, grid computing and more.

The joint, subsidiary and ancillary undertakings of TCS are as follows:

Direct Ancillary

- A. P. Online
- C. S. Technology
- C. M. C.
- Diligenta
- Exgenics Canada Incorporation
- Tata America International Corporation
- TCS Asia Pacific
- TCS Belgium S. A.
- TCS Deutschland GmBH
- TCS France S. A.
- TCS Netherlands B. V.
- TCS Sverige A. B.
- TCS Switzerland
- Tata Infotech, Singapore
- Tata Infotech, Deutschland GmBH
- TCS F. N. S.
- TCS Iberoamerica S. A.
- W. T. I. Advanced Technology
- Indirect Ancillary

- C.M.C. America Incorporation
- Swedish Indian I.T. Resources A.B.
- TCS Solution Centre S.
- TCS Argentina S.
- TCS Brazil S./C.
- TCS De Mexico S.A., De C.V.
- TCS Inversiones, Chile
- TCS De Espana
- TCS Brazil
- TCS Chile S. A.
- TCS Italia S.R.L.
- TCS Japan
- TCS Malaysia Sdn Bhd
- TCS Luxemberg S.A. Capellen
- TCS Portugal Unipessoal
- TCS Chile
- Comicrom S.A.
- Sisteco S.A.
- Sischrome S.A.
- Pentacomp S.A.
- Pentacomp Services S.A.
- Custodia De Documentos Intres
- Financial Network Services- From centres of Europe, Malaysia, Africa, Chile, and other countries
- Chang Won Investments, etc.

Headquarters of TCS is in Mumbai and it has a business spanning around 50 countries in the world. It has a training institute in Thiruvananthapuram and another institute called Data Research Development and Design Centre in Pune.

Despite the ongoing slowdown in the economic sector and the weak global industrial situation, the net profit of the company registered a growth of 19 per cent as per the data released for the first quarter of 2009-10. Compared to the same period last year, the company's revenue grew by 12 percent which is ₹ 7,207 crore.

❑❑

Tata Teleservices

Tata's services continue to serve in each sector of teleservices, be it basic telephones, cellular telephone or internet or long-distance conversations at national and international levels. International calls are executed through Videsh Sanchar Nigam Limited acquired by Tata teleservices.

Tata's engagement with the high-tech and services sector began in 1980 after Ratan Tata prepared a roadmap for entry into the sector. At that time this sector was safe for the Department of Telecommunications (DOT). The government's attitude was not firm. Tata opened up a joint venture with the Government of Kerala when the field of manufacturing of telephone equipment was opened to the private sector. Thus, Keltron was born. Tata in collaboration with a Japanese company started manufacturing PABX sets in Ahmedabad. It later contacted an American company.

In 1990, the government was ready to set up joint ventures with multinationals.

In 1995, the government invited tenders for cellular telephones in the country. Tata established a joint venture with Bell, Canada in 1997. In 1999, Tata Teleservices obtained a license to provide basic telecom services in Andhra Pradesh. Later, the company also obtained a license to work in 5 other telecom circles — Karnataka, Tamil Nadu, Delhi, Gujarat and Maharashtra. These regions represent 56 per cent of the country's customers.

TTCL with its ancillary unit Tata Tele Services (Maharashtra) serves 32 million customers in 7,500 cities and towns across the country.

In 2005, the company forayed into the mobile services sector and operates its services in 22 telecom circles in the country. Its network is considered the best in India.

Business Sector

Tata Teleservices represents the Tata group in the field of telecommunications. This occupies a leading position in the field of CDMA 1x technology, in India. The company provides services in all areas of telecommunications, be it mobile services or wireless desktop phones or public booth telephones or wireline services. Its other services are value added services like voice portal, roaming, post-paid internet services, three-way conferencing, group calling, Wi-Fi internet, tata cords, calling cords services, etc. Other products made available by the company include prepaid wireless desktop phones, public phone booths, mobile handsets, voice and data services such as games, voice portals, picture messaging, news, cricket, astrology and more.

The company along with Tata Teleservices Maharashtra is on the path to provide GSM services, which the company has planned to launch this year. Tata Indicom plays a pivotal role in providing mobile services. The company has partnered with leading telecom service providers for reliable and technologically advanced networks.

Joint Ventures, Ancillary and Subsidiaries

- Tata Teleservices (Maharashtra)
- Virgin Mobile India, based on a franchise with Virgin Mobile Group. The company is headquartered in Mumbai.

❑

Tata Communications

Tata Communications Ltd. (Formerly VSNL) international long distance, enterprise data, internet services is the largest telecom company in India. This Mumbai-based company operates in about 80 cities in 40 countries. It is the world's largest submarine cable bandwidth provider through its ancillary Tyco Global Network. Another ancillary of Tata Communications is—VSNL, Canada, formerly called 'Teleglobe', a major partner of Neotel, South Africa.

Videsh Sanchar Nigam Limited was established in 1986 as a company owned by the Government of India. In 2000, the Tata group took over the possession of its control. In 2008, it was called Tata Communications Ltd. and it announced a global expansion programme worth 2 billion US dollars.

❑

Tata Sky

It is a joint venture of Tata Group and Star TV, where Tata Group holds 80 per cent stakes while the latter holds 20 percent stakes. Although it was established only in 2004, it started functioning practically from 2006. It currently provides programmes on around 140 channels. The company uses the Sky brand of Sky Broadcasting Company of England. In 2008, the company introduced the PVR services under the banner of Tata Sky Plus, which features 45 hours of recording in MPEG-4 relative set top boxes.

❑

Titan Industries

It is a joint venture between Tata Group and Tamil Nadu Industrial Development Corporation. It is the sixth largest company in the world, which manufactures wrist watches. Watches manufactured by it include Titan, Fastrack, Sonata, Nebula and Xylys brands. Its repertoire includes watches, their accessories and jewellery. Its manufacturing units are in Hosur, Dehradun and Goa. It also manufactures jewellery under the brand name 'Tanishq'.

Titan's watch division was started in 1987. At that time, it was the third largest watch manufacturer in the country after HMT and Allwyn. Titan watches occupy 25 per cent of the market in India. It also exports watches to about 40 countries in the world through its marketing ancillary units. These ancillary units are in Singapore, Aden, Dubai and London. It has a long retail chain for marketing in the Indian market. ❑

Tanishq

Currently, Tanishq is the most prominent jewellery brand in India. It is the first brand to offer branded jewellery in India. Adorned with 22 carats pure gold jewellery, diamonds or coloured gems, it offers a wide range in the country. Tanishq was founded in 1995. It introduced new rules in the field of precious jewellery, challenging the dynastic tradition of goldsmiths. It caused excitement by entering the market with the guarantee of the purity of Tata. Only then was it found that in India, jewellery manufacturers in the name of pure gold have been fooling the general public for centuries. It made the people aware with about the prevalence of rampant corruption through its criterion of technology in the purity based on personal belief. It was the brand Tanishq, which used an advanced technique such as karat metre to provide a means of testing the purity of gold without harming the gold jewellery.

Tanishq established a production centre and base of new research in the field of jewellery making in India. Spread over an area of 1,35,000 sq ft, its large unit is equipped with modern machines and equipment. The factory set up at Hosur in Tamil Nadu centralizes the work of artisans making various styles of jewellery. On the one hand, they are artisans who are exploited by jewellery makers by making them work for low wages, while Tanishq's artisans get excellent working conditions and reasonable salaries and other facilities. This is the reason why Tanishq makes great progress today and its marketing branches have opened in many cities.

❑❑

Tata Technologies

Tata Technologies is a Tata group company that works in the automotive industry and provides engineering and design solutions. In 2005, the company took control of Incat, of Europe, a major company operating in the same area. The headquarters of Tata Technologies Ltd. is located near Pune. The company operates its operations in the US and Europe through its wholly owned ancillary units, which are in Detroit, Denver and London. The company also does business in Thailand.

❑

Voltas Limited

This Mumbai-based Tata company is primarily an engineering, air conditioning and refrigeration company. It is engaged in a large area of industries such as heating, air conditioning, refrigeration, ventilation, electromechanical projects, machine tools, textile machinery, construction equipment, mining, water management, etc.

❑

Tata AIG

Tata AIG General is a joint venture between the Tata Group and American International Group (AIG). This led to the combination of Tata Group's prominence and AIG making its global presence (in the insurance and finance services sector) in India. The Tata group holds 74 per cent stake in this venture and AIG holds 26 per cent. Tata AIG's General Insurance Company started its business in India in 2001. It provides services in each sector of general insurance such as motor, home, accident and health, travel, energy, marine, property liability and many other specialized financial sectors.

AIG is the world's leading business group in the field of insurance and finance services. AIG Units offer their services to commercial, institutional and individual customers. Apart from these, AIG also ranks highest in the world in the fields of companies, retirement services, financial and asset management services. AIG is listed on the Stock Exchange of New York, Paris, Tokyo, and Switzerland.

❑

The Taj Group

Jamsetji Tata had four main plans in mind, which he wanted to fulfil in his lifetime. They were—steel, hydroelectric power, a research university, and a hotel compared to no other hotel in Asia. He wanted to build a world class hotel in Bombay. Only this wish could be fulfilled during his lifetime when the magnificent Taj Mahal Hotel was inaugurated in 1903 in Bombay. Today the Taj is the synonym of hospitality. The Taj is the best in the world in terms of customer satisfaction and has opened training centres for excellent training of its employees.

At the 'World Travel Ceremony' held in Kuala Lumpur (Malaysia), the Taj Mahal Hotel, Mumbai was unanimously declared the best hotel in the Asia-Pacific region by all travel agents in the world.

In Kerala, the Taj has started a project called 'Green Tourism', where specialist Ayurvedic treatment is available in five hotels of the Taj Group.

The Taj Mahal Palace and Tower, Mumbai have made history since its inauguration in 1903. Many Maharajas, princes, presidents and other prominent personalities have received hospitality at the Taj.

The Taj is also an excellent specimen of architecture which offers a fascinating view of the Arabian Sea and the Gateway of India. Besides foreign crafts and techniques there is extensive use of Indian crafts and artifacts in it.

As a result of additional construction, the number of rooms in the hotel doubled, in 1970. The tower wing was speculated by a noted American sculptor named Melton Bekker. Dale Keller, a Swiss designer from Hong Kong, was in charge of its interiors. Indian essence was kept alive in it by giving a special touch like the Udaipur style relief panels, Tanjore style columns, Indian restaurants, etc. In 1990, the rooms on the top four floors were modernized again.

For almost a century, the Taj Mahal Palace has become a kind of store house for a variety of paintings and artistic objects from all over the world. These items are displayed in profusion here.

Services

The Taj Mahal Palace & Tower has 565 rooms and 46 suites and its facilities are also of excellent standard. It also provides personal butler service for the Taj Club room and suites. These butlers play an important role as a guide and assistant here.

Hotel business services include wireless Internet and broadband Internet access, colour copiers, in-house conferencing, mobile, laptops and portable printers on rent; translation, interpreters and secretarial services are also available on rent; and multimedia computers are also available. Other services include 24-hour dining, baby-sitting, beauty salon, car hire, currency exchange, dry cleaning, florist, house doctor, laundry and travel services.

The Taj and the Attack of 26/11: On November 26, 2008, two of the big hotels in Bombay were attacked by Pakistani terrorists, the Taj Mahal Palace and Tower Hotel was also one of them where the terrorists caused immense destruction. Overall, there was considerable loss of life and property. The 31 people who died here included the staff along with the guests. Till the time Mumbai was freed from the clutches of the terrorists after a siege of more than 59 hours, they had killed 183 people and wounded 239 people in 10 places in total.

The Taj was in bad shape. Blood-soaked rooms and corridors, gunshot holes, grenades ravages and burnt interiors. Many Taj employees, including guests and security personnel, also lost their lives. The Taj's general manager's wife and two children also died in the fire. But like the people of Mumbai, the Taj employees also did not lose courage and pledged to bring the Taj back to a dignified place.

Re-welcoming of Guests in the Taj: The Taj Mahal Palace Hotel reopened on December 21, 2008, twenty-four days after the terrorist attack, and guests began arriving. By December 21, booking was completed in all its restaurants. On the occasion of the reopening of the hotel, Ratan Tata remembered the guests and security personnel who lost their lives in the terrorist attack and also thanked the employees who wrote a new chapter by saving the lives of others risking their own lives.

The Tree of Life: A memorial called 'The Tree of Life' was also released in memory of those who lost their lives in the hotel, in the attacks of 26/11. Based on this, the names of those 31 people were recorded, so that they will always be remembered. The basis of this monument is the artwork of Jaidev Baghel, which was installed near the steps of the fifth floor, where it was found unshaken by the terrorist attack in its former position.

After this terror attack, the Taj established a fund to help not only the people who lost their lives in the Taj Hotel but also the victims of other parts of the city and the families of the deceased.

In this terrorist attack, many employees of the army, police, fire service, hotel, guests and general public also lost their lives and many were injured. Well-wishers from India as well as from outside India sent their best wishes to restore the hotel and provide relief to the victims.

Taj Public Service Welfare Trust

In response, the Taj group set up the Taj Public Service Welfare Trust. Its main objective was to provide immediate relief to the victims of the attack and the relatives of the deceased, be it ordinary people, security forces personnel or Taj employees or people from other institutions suffering from terror. This trust will continue to serve the victims of violence, natural calamities and other maleficent events in the years to come.

Apart from India Hotels Company Ltd. Sir Dorabji Tata Trust, Sir Ratan Tata Trust also approved valuable initial contributions in it. Consent from the government was also considered for contributions from foreign donors.

A board of trustees was also formed for this, which included Sir Ratan Tata, N.A. Sunavala, A.P. Goyal, R.K. Krishnakumar, R.N. Bickson and A.K. Mukerjee.

Ratan Tata worked patiently in this difficult time of the terrorist attack; but he was very upset by the negligence of the state machinery, the lateness and the lack of coordination among government agencies. While expressing his thoughts on taking responsibility for himself, people and institutions, he expressed his dissatisfaction clearly and well.

❑

Large Acquisitions of the Tata Group Across the Sea

Since 2000, the Tata Group companies have acquired many big companies abroad. Their account is as follows-

- **Year 2000:** England's tea company Tetley was acquired by Tata Tea. The acquisition was concluded for $ 43.2 million. The acquisition made Tata Tea the world's largest packaged tea company.
- **February 2004:** Tata Motors signed an agreement to acquire the commercial vehicle unit from South Korea's Daewoo Group. It cost $ 102 million.
- **August 2004:** Tata Steel Limited purchased the Steel Miller NatSteel Ltd. of Singapore for $286 million.
- **June 2005:** Tata Coffee bought America's Eight O'Clock coffee company from Gryphon Investors.
- **July 2005:** Telecom Company Videsh Sanchar Nigam Limited (VSNL) purchased the Teleglobe International Holdings Ltd. of America for $ 239 million and Tyco International Global Under Sea fibre optic cable network unit for $ 13.0 million.
- **Year 2006:** Tata Tea bought 30 per cent stake of American Water Firm Energy Brand Incorporation for $ 67.7 million and sold it to Coca-Cola within a year for $1.2 billion.
- **January 2007:** Tata Steel acquired Anglo-Dutch steel maker Corus Group for $ 12 billion. This was the largest acquisition by an Indian company abroad so far.

- **March 2007:** Tata Power bought two coal mines in Indonesia for $ 1.3 billion.
- **January 2008:** Tata Chemicals acquired the American soda ash manufacturing company, General Chemical Industrial Products Inc. for $1.01 billion.
- **March 26, 2008:** Tata Motors succeeded in acquiring the luxury brands Land Rover and Jaguar of the British company Ford Motors. The deal was concluded for US $ 2.3 billion.

In addition, in recent times Tata Advanced Systems has tied up with a US-based helicopter manufacturer, Sikorsky, to manufacture helicopters. Under this, 19-seater S-92 helicopters will be built. The agreement was concluded for $ 350 million. The helicopters were available for delivery from 2010.

❑

Some Important Achievements

Ratan Tata has amazing management capabilities. He knows the value of time and makes decisions accordingly. He also had to face failures, but did not lose courage. He learned the mantra to climb the steps of success through his failures.

Acquisition of Steel Company Corus

'Corus' emerged in 1999, when British Steel merged with its rival Dutch steel company Hoogovens. The Corus employed 47,300 employees, including 24,000 at its various sites in the UK—Port Talbot, Scunthorpe and Rotherham.

Over the past few years, there was a significant reduction in its profit due to increase in raw material prices and rise in energy expenditure both in the UK and Netherlands. Therefore, it was forced to join an institute whose production cost was low. When the sale of the Corus Steel Plant was decided, the big companies of the steel sector came into the fray. Tata Steel of Ratan Tata was also one of them. But then it was not considered to be a strong buyer. All kinds of thoughts were in the air. The first was that Ratan Tata is not a serious contender, the second was that the Corus purchase would prove to be a losing deal for him. But Ratan Tata kept quiet at that time. He had made up his mind on what had to be done. It was not in his nature to retreat after making decisions, no matter what the challenge. The same happened in this case. In the acquisition of Corus, he got a huge challenge from the Brazilian firm CSN.

The deal between Corus and CSN would have produced the fifth largest steel company in the world, with an annual production of 24 million tonnes. This would allow Corus access to low-cost and high-quality cast iron, which was available at the Casa de Pedra mine of CSN. Along with this, it would also have access to the fast-emerging markets of South America.

Whether the deal was with Tata or CSN in both cases, the new company would become the fifth largest steel producer in the world and it went into foreign ownership only a decade after becoming the British steel company Corus.

The Tata group joined the acquisition movement with an offer of 455 pence per share. Along with Brazilian CSN, Russia's Severstal was also interested in its acquisition. The Corus Board put its bid at 4.3 billion pounds. Severstal later expressed his reluctance to take over, but CSN raised its bid to 475 pence per share. Meanwhile, there was intense discussion between CSN and Corus on the issue that a proposal of 500 pence per share came from Tata, which proved to be a serious setback for both. Both were quite surprised, but CSN raised its bid to 515 pence per share.

Corus is Europe's second-largest steel producer, with 12 billion pounds of annual revenue, crude steel production of over 20 million tonnes, that is mainly produced in England and the Netherlands.

The Corus consists mainly of three operating divisions—Striped products, long products and distribution and building systems. It has its own network of global sales offices and service centres, employing approximately 42,000 people.

Corus is a major supplier in the world's developed market. Its goods are supplied to the manufacturing, automotive, packaging, mechanical and electrical engineering, metal goods and oil and gas sectors.

After the acquisition, Corus is now an ancillary of Tata Steel. Today Tata Steel has business in about 50 countries around the world, including Corus, Tata Steel, Thailand and

Nat Steel Asia. Around 80,000 employees are employed for the Tata Steel Group in five continents of the world. The crude steel production capacity of the group is estimated at 28 million tonnes.

It is estimated that by 2011-12, the combined production capacity of Tata Steel and Corus will be 40 million tonnes and the total turnover will reach $ 32 billion. This acquisition is the largest acquisition by an Indian company abroad.

The bid for the acquisition lasted for eight rounds. Brazil's CSN made its final offer bid up to 603 pence per share. Tata Steel made the bid in its favour by offering 5 pence more, i.e. 608 pence per share. Therefore, the last bet was in the name of Tata, which did not lower its own and the country's head and thus created a new history.

❑

Acquisition of Jaguar Land Rover

Jaguar, founded in 1922, is the world's leading luxury and sports car manufacturer. Land Rover has been working in this sector since 1948. Jaguar Land Rover is made up of two big British car brands and its manufacturing units are located in England.

The company has over 16,000 employees, of which around 3,500 are engineers. It has manufacturing units in Whitley and Geydon, UK.

Three models of Jaguar- XF, XJ and XK, are manufactured at Birmingham plant and those of Land Rover-Defender, Discovery-3, Rover Sport, etc, are manufactured at Solihull.

This business is a great means for England to earn money. Seventy-eight per cent of Land Rover cars are exported to 169 countries. On the other hand, 70 per cent of Jaguars are exported to 63 countries. Importers and franchise sellers are resorted to for sale to customers.

On March 26, 2008, Tata Motors purchased the Jaguar Land Rover business from Ford Motor Company for US $ 2.3 billion. Many companies of the world tried to buy these famous brands, but only Ratan Tata was successful.

Ratan Tata himself was present at the Jaguar Land Rover headquarters in Gaydon at the post-acquisition transfer ceremony. Leading officers were present on behalf of the acquired company.

Speaking on the occasion, Ratan Tata said that this was a memorable moment for Tata Motors. Jaguar and Land Rover are the two big British brands, which have a global market and have substantial growth potential. Ratan Tata observed: "Jaguar Land Rover team will have our full support. The company will continue to have its own personal identity. Similarly, it will continue to work in accordance with its previously targeted business objectives."

In the procurement regime, royalty-free continuous ownership of the intellectual property rights construction plant, two design centres in England and a global network of national sales companies, were given to the Jaguar Land Rover.

A long-term agreement has been signed for the supply of engines, stamping and spare parts to Jaguar Land Rover. Other areas of cooperation by Ford will be the availability of information technology, accounting and testing facilities. The two companies will continuously cooperate in the field of design and development. Ford Motor Company will continue to provide financial assistance to Jaguar Land Rover buyers and customers for a duration in the transition period.

The deal will provide an important opportunity for Tata Motors to establish a strong footprint in the international automobile sector. With this, Tata Motors which was earlier known only for manufacturing low-cost cars will be able to make a mark in the luxury car category.

The deal also appeared as a major relief for the Ford company, as a lot of money was being spent on the creation of these two luxurious brands and the expenditure exceeded the income. On the other hand, it was not able to get sufficient customers. As a result, the company incurred heavy losses for the last two-three years.

❑

Entry of Land Rover Cars in the Indian Market

Almost a year after the acquisition, Tata Motors launched the Jaguar Land Rover car in the Indian market in the last week of June 2009. The three cars of the Rover models—Discovery-3, Range Rover and Sport—can each cost between ₹ 65 lakhs and ₹ 1 crore.

While introducing these luxury cars to Indian customers, Ratan Tata said, "With this, Land Rover brand cars have entered India." Although it had entered here in the past years, but the relationship with the customers here was severed in a few years. Even after the acquisition by Tata, during the economic downturn, its sales fell by one-third as compared to earlier sales, during the last one year. Keeping this in mind, Ratan Tata said, "Jaguar Land Rover could not be praised in times of economic recession, but they are excellent products with their superb production. After coming out of the recession, we can say that it was a difficult decision to take ownership of it. But as an Indian, I am proud to be the owner of these brands. We will definitely bring back their lost dignity.

Several prominent officials including Jaguar Land Rover Chief Executive Officer David Smith were present on this occasion in Mumbai. Jaguar Land Rover series can be compared to Mercedes-S, Audi-6, BMW-7, etc.

With the entry of Jaguar Land Rover, Tata Motors has become a company engaged in the business of expensive luxury cars as well as low-cost cars for the common people.

❑

Chairman of Tata Sons

1. Jamsetji Tata (Year 1887-1904)
2. Sir Dorabji Tata (Year 1904-1932)
3. Sir Nowroji Saklatwala (Year 1932-1938)
4. J.R.D. Tata (Year 1938-1991)
5. Ratan Naval Tata (Year 1991-2010)

❑

Tata Group: Some Facts

- **Founded:** In the year 1868, Owned by Tata Sons, Founded by Jamsetji Tata.
- **Promoter Companies:** Tata Sons and Tata Industries.
- **Headquarters:** Bombay House, 24 Homi Mody Street, Mumbai.
- **Business Sector:** Materials, Engineering, Energy, Chemicals and Consumer Products, Information Systems and Communications.
- **Revenue of Group:** $62.5 billion (Rs. 2,51,543 crore) (Source: Year 2007-08).
- **Profit:** $5.4 billion (Rs 21,578 crore).
- **Number of Share Holders:** More than 32 lakhs.
- **Number of Companies:** 96 operating companies.
- **Number of Employees:** 3,50,000 employees.
- **International Condition:** Businesses in about 80 countries of the world.
- **International Revenue:** 38.3 billion dollars. 61 percent of the group's total revenue.
- **Companies Listed on the Bombay Stock Exchange:** 27 Companies.
- **Companies Listed on the New York Stock Exchange:** Two- Tata Motors and Tata Communications.

Management Board

Ratan Naval Tata, Chairman Tata Sons.

Members of Group Corporate Centre

- N.A. Sunawala. Vice-Chairman, Tata Sons.
- J.J. Irani, Director, Tata Sons.
- R.K. Krishnakumar, Director, Tata Sons.
- R. Gopalkrishnan, Executive Director, Tata Sons.
- Ishaat Hussain, Finance & Executive Director, Tata Sons.
- Kishore Chaukar, Managing Director, Tata Industries.
- Arun Gandhi, Executive Director, Tata Sons.
- Alan Rosling, Executive Director, Tata Sons.

Commercial Importance

- **Tata Steel:** The sixth largest steel producer in the world and the largest steel producer in the private sector in India.
- **TCS:** Asia's largest software manufacturer.
- **Tata Tea:** The world's largest integrated tea company.
- **Tata Chemicals:** Largest in India and third largest soda ash producer in the world.
- **Tata Power:** India's largest energy company in the private sector.
- **Taj Group:** The largest chain of five-star luxury hotels in India.
- **Titan:** The world's fifth largest watch manufacturer.

First in India

- Establishment of the steel industry.

- Envisage and implement labour-friendly rules, such as 8 hours of work, provident fund, gratuity, maternity benefit and all other facilities.
- Establishment of India's first power plant.
- Establishment of civil aviation.
- Start of insurance business.
- To establish a chain of luxury hotels in India.
- Production of commercial vehicles.
- Software development work.
- Production of Indica, the indigenous car of India.

❑

Honours Received by Ratan Tata

- On January 26, 2008, he was awarded India's second highest civilian honour the 'Padma Vibhushan'.
- In 2008, he was awarded the 'NASSCOM Global Leadership Award-2008'.
- In 2007, Ratan Tata received the 'Carnegie Medal of Philanthropy' Award from the Tata family.
- In 2006, Cornell University honoured him with the 26th 'Robert S. Hetfield Fellow in Economics'.
- In 2004, Ratan Tata was awarded the title of 'Honorary Economic Advisor to Hangzhou City' in China.
- He has received the titles of honorary doctorate from London School of Economics and Indian Institute of Technology, Kharagpur.
- In May 2008, he was ranked in *Time* magazine's list of 100 influential people in the world.
- On August 29, 2008, the Government of Singapore granted him Honorary Citizenship. The award was conferred on him for his contribution to the development of Singapore.

Earned Membership

- Member, Prime Minister's Council, Trade and Industry.
- Member, Advisory Board, Mitsubishi Corporation.

- Member, American International Group, J.P. Morgan and Booz Allen Hamilton.
- Member, Board of Trustees, RAND Corporation.
- Member, University of Southern California, Cornell University.
- Member, South Africa International Investment Council.
- Member, Asia-Pacific Advisory Committee on New York Stock Exchange.
- President, Indian Institute of Science Court, Bangalore.
- Secretary, Managing Committee, Tata Institute of Fundamental Research, Mumbai.
- Member, Global Business Council of HIV; For AIDS awareness related work in India.

Along with this he is associated with many other national and international organizations.

❑❑

Paramount in Generosity

The money that Jamsetji and his sons earned during the industrialization of the country was not spent on their comfort and luxury. He invested most of that money in the trusts for the welfare of the people, so that it can be used only for their welfare.

Earning money for yourself and earning for others are both opposite poles. But here the mention is of that business family which has earned money for its country through all the struggles, troubles and dangers and has formed and efficiently operated many trusts to spend it in the service of compatriots in various ways.

Jamsetji's Social Welfare Works

The group which Jamsetji Tata started with the establishment of a textile factory in central India in 1870, is now famous in the country and abroad. Jamsetji's thought and vision led to the foundation of the textile industry as well as the steel and energy industries in the country. He laid the foundation for technical education, started public welfare works and thus paved the way for India to reach the gateway of the twenty-first century.

After Jamsetji's death, his elder son Sir Dorabji Tata took charge of the Tata group and with the support his younger brother Sir Ratan Tata and uncle R.D. Tata he gave form to Jamsetji's dream.

The spirit of trusteeship is a by-product of the business of Jamsetji and his sons, through which they had to meet the needs of the country. His extensive ideological thinking gave him the idea of doing something beyond his business interests and the determination to give a concrete form to it. The desire to develop his country as an industrialized nation was deeply rooted in Jamsetji. Along with this, he was filled with the passion to train the youth of our country. With this idea, from 1892 onwards, he started sending deserving youth to study abroad by awarding scholarships for higher education. When the British opened up the Indian Civil Service (equivalent to today's Indian Administrative Service) to the Indians for recruitment, it was his heartfelt desire that more Indians should join it. So he started giving scholarships to the worthy people. A survey in 1924 made it clear that out of every 5 Indian ICS at that time, one was a Tata Scholar. Among the people who were benefited from the Tata Endowment Fund at that time, a few are: J.C. Koyaji,a member of the Viceroy's Executive, B.N. Rao, Chief Justice Bombay High Court, Dr. Jeevaraj N. Mehta (later Chief Minister of Gujarat), Dr. Raja Ramanna, K.R. Narayanan (later became President of India), V.V. Narlikar, J.V. Narlikar, etc.

❑❑

Contribution of Sir Ratan Tata

Jamsetji was fortunate in the fact that his sons also had similar rites. His younger son Ratan Tata was very kind and generous hearted and was always prepared to help any individual or institution in trouble. The national sentiment had merged with his personal views. He was a man of extensive and balanced views.

Charity or philanthropy is possible only when there is passion inside the person and he is deeply attached to any thought and action. Then only would he be willing to give time to it as well as cooperate and help financially. During his lifetime, Sir Ratan Tata had identified many cases where according to him there was need of cooperation and help.

Gopalkrishna Gokhale founded the 'Servants of India Society' in Poona in June 1905. His aim was to prepare selfless, intelligent workers for India. Such workers, who can devote their lives to the service of the country.

At the request of Gopalkrishna Gokhale, Sir Ratan Tata gave assistance of ₹ 10,000 every year to Gopalkrishna Gokhale's organization for ten years. This amount was to be spent by the institution for the welfare of the weaker sections of the society.

Similarly, he also helped the non-cooperation movement being run by Mahatma Gandhi in South Africa. This movement was being carried out on the apartheid policy of the then British Government and the issue of mistreatment of the people of the Indian community. Like other patriots,

Sir Ratan also believed that it was a legitimate and cooperative movement. The repression movement by the British government was in full swing against it.

On the appeal of cooperation by Mahatma Gandhi, Sir Ratan sent a sum of ₹ 1.25 lakh in instalments for five years from 1909 to 1913 to Gandhiji so that he could continue his movement.

Expressing his gratitude to Sir Ratan, Gandhiji said that his cooperation has led to the realization that India has now woken up. His help will prove to be a great force for our movement.

In 1912, Sir Ratan Tata proposed to help the University of London to set up a bench that suggested the causes of poverty and ways to overcome them. A plan was submitted by the university. A Chair (Peeth) was established in 1913 after Sir Ratan Tata's approval. Sir Ratan agreed to pay 1,400 pounds annually for this project for three years. In 1916, it was extended for the next five years. Even after the death of Sir Ratan Tata, the trust formed in his name continued to grant this bench till 1931. In these nineteen years, many scholars of the university did research work on the status of workers in various occupations and got it published. Today the 'Sir Ratan Tata Foundation' is a permanent institution at the London School of Economics.

Between 1913 and 1917, Sir Ratan gave an economic grant of ₹ 75,000 to implement the archaeological mining project of Pataliputra. As a result of this excavation, many items of archaeological importance were revealed. Items received are displayed in Patna's museum. This was his immense urge to bring national pride to the fore.

Sir Ratan Tata was also an admirer of art and culture. He was also an enthusiastic traveller, who travelled to many places in the country and abroad. During his travels, he collected many items of art and cultural importance. In 1919, the collection was valued at ₹ 5 lakhs. After his death, according to his will this entire collection was transferred to the Prince of Wales Museum in 1921, where it is still on display.

This is just a specimen of the fulfilment of the social concerns of Sir Ratan. During his lifetime he did many works of philanthropy. These include assistance to victims of disasters like floods, famine, fire, earthquakes, etc. and periodic assistance to hospitals, monuments, schools and many other social utility institutions.

His approach on how to use a trust fund was quite clear. In 1913, he put forward an outline of it. According to him, the fields of education, teaching and industry were within its scope and all the things of general public work were included in it. The employment of persons who were suitable and capable in reaching the depth of cases for social, economic and political fulfilment was its other feature. Along with this, he would agree to support any plan and experiment only when it was carefully prepared and considered in all aspects.

❑

Sir Ratan Tata Trust

After the death of Sir Ratan Tata in 1918, the Sir Ratan Tata Trust was set up with ₹ 80 lakh. It is one of the oldest grantors in India. After his death, the public welfare works carried out by him were continued by the trust formed in his name.

In 1995, a strategy was prepared for the activities of the Sir Ratan Tata Trust from 1995 to 2000 under the leadership of Ratan Tata. It had to do something beyond the traditional welfare works so that the welfare works could be planned for national development.

For this, it was decided to focus on the following areas to provide grants—

- Rural Living and Community Areas
- Education
- Health
- Arts and culture
- Public initiative.

Under this, around 65 new grants were approved for the year 2000-2001 and the trust sanctioned grants worth about 16 crores for various works. This is just one example. In later years, the number of schemes offered and its monetary size increased.

After the introduction of the new strategy by Ratan Tata, the Trust has provided major support to programmes to improve the standard of living of the rural poor and the rural community.

Under this, special attention is being paid to the following areas-

- Non-agricultural works, help to the women's groups notably.
- Rural community.
- Relief to communities suffering from natural disasters.
- Research on major problems in rural area.
- Emphasis on development of human resources in rural areas.
- Emphasis on proper management of resources to increase agricultural production.

In the field of education, the trust is focused on two main categories — 1. Schooling, 2. Higher education. The objective of the grants has been to support community education in this area. The main emphasis is also on quality education. It is an attempt to achieve this by increasing the level of knowledge of teachers by training and by paying adequate attention to the education being imparted in the classrooms. To keep the children in schools, various programmes are being provided outside schools as well. Special attention is also being given to value-based education.

The Trust supports community-based health programmes in the health sector. For this, attention is also being given to cooperation of public and individual joint ventures and to develop an activist organization of public health professionals.

Various types of grants are given to the art sector by the Sir Ratan Tata Trust for the safety and security of things of archaeological importance.

The Trust also supports such programmes in which people of both male and female sections are being made capable according to the changing social changes.

The trust provides grants to institutions working in some selected areas. The condition of the grant is only that the work has the desired effect on the society or it is a work of an important nature in some area.

Along with the institutions, the trust also gives grants to individual people and small institutions. This work is being done by 'Sir Ratan Tata Small Grants Programme'. In this, grants are given mainly to small institutions engaged in welfare works and people working for educational and health purposes.

❑

Sir Dorabji Tata Trust

Sir Dorabji Tata Trust was established in 1932 by Dorabji, the elder son of Jamsetji Tata. Shortly before his death, Dorabji had bequeathed this trust to his entire estate, which at that time was ₹ 1 crore. It included his significant stakes of Tata Sons.

Although Sir Dorabji spent most of his time in fulfilling his father's big dreams, he still had time for public welfare works. One of the two trusts he founded three months before his death was the Lady Tata Memorial Trust. It was of relatively small stature and was primarily for research in the area of leukemia. The second Sir Dorabji Tata Trust was on a large and ambitious scale. It was due to the generosity of this trust that some of the leading institutions of India were established, such as-

1. Tata Institute of Social Sciences (1936).
2. Tata Memorial Hospital (1941).
3. Tata Institute of Fundamental Research (1945).
4. National Centre for Performing Arts (1966).

After the death of J.R.D., honouring his wish the Dorabji Tata Trust helped the M.S. Swaminathan Research Foundation to establish the J.R.D. Tata Centre for Ecotechnology.

Jamsetji Tata had a strong desire to establish a 'School of Medical Research into Tropical Medicine'. Dorabji wanted to establish it in 1912 to honour his wish. But for some reasons this could not be possible then. The wish of the two was fulfilled in 1999, when the 'Sir Dorabji Tata Centre for Research in Tropical Diseases' was established at the Indian Institute of Science, Bangalore. In 2004, the Trust contributed to the establishment of the School of Rural Development, Tuljapur and Tata Medical Centre, Calcutta. From its beginning till 2006, the Trust distributed approximately ₹ 380 crores and all this was given to support creative work.

Apart from this, Tata Trusts contribute to many areas in different parts of the country. A series of Tata trusts will be sufficient to demonstrate their work and scope. These are:

- Sir Ratan Tata Trust.
- Sir Dorabji Tata Trust.
- Jamsetji Tata Trust.
- J.N. Tata endowment.
- J.R.D. Tata Trust.
- The J.R.D. and Thelma J. Tata Trust.
- Lady Meherbai D. Tata Education Trust.
- Lady Tata Memorial Trust.
- R. D. Tata Trust.
- M.K. Tata Trust.
- Tata Social Welfare Trust.
- Tata Education Trust.

The Tata group companies are also engaged at their levels in developing their surroundings and making lives of people happier. Not only this, they are involved in public welfare works even in remote areas of the country outside their region.

❑

Relief Work During Disasters

Tata's tradition of relief work during natural disasters began with the earthquake in Quetta in 1934. The specialty of the relief work done by Tata is that whether it is relief work or rehabilitation, they do all the work themselves with their own resources and through their people.

One example will be sufficient. In 1993, there was a great earthquake in Latur in the morning and a supreme meeting was called the same day in the evening for relief work. But before the meeting itself, several groups of Tata employees had departed with adequate furnishings and materials to provide relief to the people of the earthquake-affected area. Where else can one find such passion? Other employees donated blood for the victims. On this front, the Tata Relief Committee set up for the eastern part of the country, helped the earthquake victims just like the relief committee of its western part. The Relief Committee of the Western Region took up various relief and rehabilitation schemes and completed them. To live in these, construction of residential buildings, establishment of schools and establishment of health centres are the main. The Sir Dorabji Tata Trust undertook the task of establishing water facilities and improving the condition of agriculture and animals. Through the Relief and Rehabilitation Division of his Tata Relief Committee, Ratan Tata helped the government of Gujarat by constructing 22 schools in the earthquake-affected Rapar taluka of Kutch. These school buildings are built to the best of engineering standards and are seismic.

Even during the Kargil War, as per its practice, Tata chose the path of functional cooperation, rather than merely concluding his duty by paying a cheque. Tata consulted the Ministry of Defence and set up a special Tata Defence Welfare Corps Fund in the Ministry of Defence. In this, companies and employees of the Tata group donated an amount of ₹ 12 crore.

This amount was not only to help the martyred or injured in Kargil or their family members, but also to help the victims of other wars and conflicts before it. It was also for the soldiers of the security forces who were in the Sri Lanka conflict, counter insurgency, peace keeping work and those who became crippled due to war; for widows of the martyrs and for giving grants for the higher education of their children. The officers of Tata and the Security Army used to meet for necessary allocation every 6 months.

Ratan Tata is the chairman of the multi-purpose trusts of the Tata Group. The idea of creative work for Tata philanthropy is a revolutionary idea for the traditional charitable organizations whose work was only to donate. Today, the 'Tata family' is one of the family among the few philanthropists in the country, which is involved in the development of the country, battling with problems at the individual, local and national levels. Along with helping in the development of the country, Ratan Tata is associated with all the welfare works.

❑

Nano: Manufacturing of the People's Car

The world's cheapest car project began in 2003 under Ratan Tata, chairman of Tata Motors. Ratan Tata got this inspiration from the troubles of millions of two-wheeler drivers who could not afford expensive cars. Therefore, take necessary travels with their family of 3-4 members on a two-wheeler. In this way, they complete their journey by risking not only their own life but also of their entire family. Ratan Tata had a dream to build and deliver a car within their budget to ease their troubles. Tata made the necessary changes to the manufacturing process to meet its design criteria to make a low-budget car possible, emphasizing innovation and it asked the suppliers to give form to new design concepts. The car was designed keeping in mind the changes suggested by Ratan Tata. As compared to the Maruti-800, the Nano has 21 percent more space inside it. According to CRISIL Rating Agency, the entry of Nano into the market would expand India's car business by 65 percent. Tata Motor has kept the initial price of the Nano at ₹ 1,00,000, hence it has also been called Lakhtakia car. It is the lowest priced car in the world. It can also be purchased by families with an annual income of ₹ 1 lakh. In this sense it is actually a people's car.

Tata Motors showcased the Nano model at the Ninth Auto Expo on January 10, 2008. Due to the relatively low price and other features, it was the centre of attraction.

The Tata Nano is a small four-seater city car. Its engine is installed in the rear. It has been greatly appreciated due to its low price and environmental relative characteristics. The main idea is that the Tata group will produce the Nano on a large scale, especially its electric model. Along with sales in India, it will be exported worldwide. The car will be produced in one standard and two luxury models. This project to manufacture the world's cheapest car started in 2003 on the initiative of the Chairman of Tata Motors, Ratan Tata. The success of Tata Motors in the production of a mini truck in 2005 also inspired the development of Nano.

Tata's initial goal was to produce the world's least expensive car, with a starting price of ₹ 100,000 and 2,300 dollars in US dollars. This price remained despite the fact that the material price had risen by 13 to 23 percent within five years of developing the car.

Tata Nano's electric model is also expected to be in great demand overseas. Director General for Energy and Transport, European Commission Matthias Ruete is of the view that the entire continent of Europe, like other countries, is eagerly awaiting the commercial marketing of Tata Nano. But considering the adverse effect of carbon dioxide on the environment, it would be more appropriate to develop an electric model of Nano.

Launch of the Nano Project

In fact, the Nano project started in 2003 when Tata Motors formed a team of four members and asked them to complete a new project. The project was the development of a new four-wheeler traffic vehicle. At that time it was only declared that it would cost ₹ 1,00,000. At that time the lowest priced car cost around ₹ 2.5 lakhs. It was also clarified that the trust and safety of the customers and environmental requirements have to be taken care of in this.

The design team considered several designs and looked at alternative methods of vehicle manufacturing and tried to draw some conclusions from the then small cars.

The team considered a number of options and situations, such as the use of plastic instead of metal, the decrease of internal space or the use of a low power engine. The focus at that time was to keep the price low. Various techniques were tried. But a question remains incomplete on how much the customer will be satisfied. When it was decided that the autorickshaw approach would not work for the development of a suitable car, other ideas emerged, such as- Doorless, where there is an iron door, cloth ceiling, plastic doors, etc.

But Ratan Tata did not agree to any of these suggestions. He had a clear idea that a whole car was needed at a low price, not a car-like structure.

Many ideas were tried. Headlights in a different shape, to give the front part of the car a child-like appearance—big eyes in a small face, etc. But Ratan Tata asked for something different. Repeated changes in the design was painful for the team.

A feature of New Indica was added to the Nano. This led to a change in the front volume of the Nano and with it a noticeable change was seen in the look of the car.

This was a delightful turn in the development of the car, as well as a director. Keeping in mind that the car should look big too and the wheels on the corners should give the car an attractive look on the road, a full-fledged shape was developed. Discussions were made on even the shape and location of the lower corner of the glass. In all these matters, discussions with Ratan Tata continued.

By July 2007, a model was almost settled and an idea to work on it was formulated at the initial stage. That's when Tata found the front of the car somewhat awkward, so he decided to increase it. A new design was made and presented to Ratan Tata in late August, the same year, which he immediately approved.

Now it was the turn of the interior design of the car. There was ample scope for changes here compared to traditional designs. Here too the question was of low cost, but there was no dispute in making it comfortable. The main task was to balance the cost of the car to suit customer satisfaction as well as the market. Along with this, the space inside the car had to be used in such a way that it would look attractive. Many ideas came up for this. They were implemented after enough deliberation on the proper suggestions and an attractive shape could be given to the interior of the car.

As this task was completely different from the traditional auto engineering, various problems cropped up at each step of manufacturing, such as installing the engine in the rear instead of the front. This was a unique idea which increased space inside the car, but hindered the balance problem. Some setups had to be brought forward accordingly. They were reconciled with the respective setups and then the trial tested its quality and efficiency. Reforms and trials took place if any deficiency was found. The floor channel was changed ten times to meet the prescribed parameters. Similarly, the dashboard and seats were also changed almost the same number of times. But the team was steeped in their work, because the feeling of doing something new and unique and the inspiration and direction of Ratan Tata was with them.

In fact, the idea of installing the engine of the car in the rear proved revolutionary for the design process. A team to raise resources for a 35 horse power engine suitable for city cars travelled all the countries of the world but, no such engine was found, which was within the budget of the car. Then an engine manufactured by Tata Motors itself was tested, which was not found suitable for the Nano. In the end the Fiat Bosch Electronics Company's engine eventually passed the trial for the Nano and was approved.

Installing the engine, gear box and exhaust system behind the rear seats was a difficult task. This was efficiently accomplished by the engineering team. The engineering team should also be appreciated for the fact that it designed and installed many new structures for the Nano.

A production team formed over the next few months after the design process was completed. This work was done neatly. Apart from Tata Motors, people were also taken from outside. Among them were graduate trainee engineers of IIT, Kharagpur and Jadavpur University. Overall, it was a mixed team, a combination of experience and youthful enthusiasm. This combined fresh ideas with experience and heralded a new work culture.

The car manufacturing process is a rigorous process. It is not easy to do it on your own with a few people or companies. Therefore, the role of other companies and vendors is important in this, which prepares and supplies all kinds of products required in car manufacturing. It is easy to get the work done or accomplished according to the traditional process and specifications. However, creating a new pool of vendors for a new concept car like the Nano or persuading the elders to make the products according to the needs of the car was a difficult task, which was resolved by communicating with them and by providing the necessary technology, design and guidance. Therefore, a group of about 100 vendors was formed to support Nano production which could design and supply products according to the need and could form part of the Nano production process and make the production of cars on a large scale possible.

❑

Singur Land Acquisition Dispute

Tata Motors chose West Bengal to set up the Nano project. This could pave the way for the establishment of industries in West Bengal along with providing employment to a large number of people. People's income would have increased, because many other industries were likely to be established there, excited by the success of the Nano project. It could eradicate and eliminate poverty for many rural people by providing employment.

Land for the establishment of the factory was acquired in the Singur region of Bengal. This process of land acquisition went well and the land owners were also satisfied with the amount of compensation. But during this process, a section of landowners, who did not live there, some illiterate farmers and activists of the Trinamool Congress, a political party, raised a dispute by refusing to accept this compensation amount. Due to the spread of politics, many new dimensions started giving vent to this dispute. Some started calling it a fertile agricultural land, while a few others began a hue and cry on the compensation of a lower amount. While some questioned the legitimacy of the acquisition of land, some made it a matter of forcibly acquiring it.

Although, the West Bengal government whole-heartedly wanted the Nano project to take place in its state. It created the necessary environment for this and facilitated the acquisition of about 997 acres of land.

Mamata Banerjee's Trinamool Congress and Socialist Unity Centre were at the forefront in opposing the land acquisition. He was given full support by civil and human rights groups, legal institutions and social workers, who are always keen to help when such opportunities arise.

Those opposing it had to face criticism and verbal warnings from the state ruling party CPI (M) and scuffles by its activists. Survey officials of the state government and Tata Motors faced heavy resistance at the hands of members of the 'Singur Krishi Bhoomi Bachao Samiti'.

As a result, the state government had to issue prohibitory orders under Section 144 of the Indian Penal Code; but the Calcutta High Court declared it illegal.

The government took control of the land earmarked for the project and began its siege in Tarabad in December 2006 amid protests. In protest to this, Mamata Banerjee called for a state-wide shutdown and later started a 25-day hunger strike. Members of her party vandalized the assembly. A large number of police forces and activists of the Marxist Party started guarding the area inside Tarabad, but the siege continued to be attacked intermittently by the opposing villagers and other groups. In January 2007, the factory construction work started on the allotted land. But the resistance against it was not being stopped, but rather it grew fierce everyday. Due to this, the work of giving practical shape to the project programme was stopped and precious time was lost.

Seeing the establishment of the Nano project fail in West Bengal, other states started efforts to pull it into their state. In the meantime, efforts were made to compromise and to find a middle path. But no effective solution was reached so that the entire project could be implemented in one place. Rather than succumb to the pressures, Ratan Tata decided to withdraw from Singur and announced it on October 2, 2008.

❑

New Centre for Setting Up the Nano Project: Sanand (Gujarat)

After spending a lot of time and resources in West Bengal, Tata announced shifting its Lakhtakia car Nano project to Sanand near Ahmedabad in Gujarat. ₹ 2,000 crores were to be spent on this project. But along with it, the decision was made to produce it from another centre for delivery of the car on time. It is another matter that before this announcement, there was a round of silent talks between the Government of Gujarat and the Tata representatives. A letter of consent was finally signed between the State Secretary of Industry and the Managing Director of Tata Motors. In this agreement, the Chief Minister of the state, Narendra Modi, also played a pivotal and effective role, who ensured the rapid allocation of 1,100 acres of good standing land. Ratan Tata himself can be thanked for this. Nearly 60 vendors, along with Tata Motors, also turned to Sanand to play a supporting role in Nano production.

It has now been decided that Tata Nano will be mass-produced from a factory set up in Sanand, Gujarat.

Meanwhile, the production of Nano started at a relatively low level at the Pantnagar plant, where some production lines of a truck were converted to conform to Nano production. Similarly, Tata Motors' Pune plant also started to work on some production lines to ensure the entry of Nano into the market at the scheduled time.

The annual production capacity of the Sanand plant will be 2,50,000 units, which will be extended later.

❑

Entry of Nano in the Market

Overcoming all the challenges, Tata Motors of Ratan Tata finally made the Nano run on the Indian roads in July 2009, when its first customer was handed the car key. Ashok Raghunath, one of the first three customers of Nano, was handed the car key by Chairman Ratan Tata himself. The colour was silver of the Nano LX model. The commencement of the process of handing over the car to customers on time despite the precious time wasted due to the Singur controversy was a favourable sign for both Nano and Tata Motors.

Nano: Some facts

Technical and Other Features

- Rear wheel drive.

- Two-cylinder 623 cc rear engine 33 PS. Car (single balancer shaft).
- Fuel Consumption 4.55 L / 100 km (21.97 km / L, city condition, normal 20 km / L).
- Length 3.1 m.
- Height 1.6 m.
- Width 1.5 m.

Safety: All sheet metal body, intrusion resistant doors, seat belts, tubeless tires. The car has successfully passed full frontal crash and side impact crash standards.

Environmentally Friendly: Reduced pollution levels from two-wheelers being built in India. Reduction in carbon dioxide emissions due to high fuel efficiency.

Nano has successfully passed all the standards set by the government to take vehicles on the road.

The Nano will have three models—the first standard model, two higher-end models that will fit the air conditioner. The RCX will be of 600 kg of these three early models and the LX will be of 615 and 635 kg respectively.

Nano-Europe was expected to be introduced in the market by 2011.

❑❑

Ratan Tata: A Gentle and Dignified Personality

Ratan Tata is also known for his gentleness and humility. He is counted among the leading businessmen of the world, but still with no sense of pride. He is unmarried and the entire Tata family is like a family to him. It would have been difficult for him to make time for his personal family in the preparation of this family; but instead of establishing a separate family, he has raised the entire Tata Empire as a family. He drives his own car to go to his office. He travels alone even on trips of long commercial nature. He does not like caboodle. In India he likes to fly his own plane. He is a skilled pilot. At the 'Aero India Exhibition' in 2007, he surprised everyone by flying as a co-pilot in the fighter aircraft F-16 and Boeing F-18.

His dealings with his subordinates are tempered with tenderness. Subordinates also look at him with an eye of affection and respect. In personal life, he is a fearless man with strong intentions. It is not possible to bow him down because he is firm in his thoughts. He is alert to the dangers, but does not change his path fearing them. It is his nature to accept challenges. He has established the Tata Group as a commercial superpower on the global scene. After 2003, he has made a series of acquisitions and commercial agreements.

He bought his truck manufacturing unit from South Korea's Daewoo Motors. Whether it is the case of Indonesia's largest coal mine or the steel mills of Singapore, Thailand and Vietnam, he is making his mark everywhere. In addition, he gained control of Pierre in New York, Ritz-Carlton in Boston and Campton Place in San Francisco through his Indian Hotels Group.

In 2004, he bought Tyco International's global undersea telecom cables for $ 130 million. Thus, the Tata group rose to the top of the world as an 'international call carrier'. With the purchase of British engineering firm Incat International, Tata Technologies has become a major supplier in the field of 'outsourced industrial design' to American auto and auto space companies. The subsequent acquisition of Dutch-British steel company Corus is a major achievement in itself. At one stroke, Tata Steel increased its finished product and reached out to auto makers in the US and Europe. With this registered a five-fold increase in its capacity. The market value of listed Tata companies has risen from $ 12 billion to $ 62 billion. Similarly, the sales and profit levels of the group have also gone up and it has crossed the figure of $29 billion and $2.8 billion respectively.

Tata Steel, Tata Motors and Tata Consultancy Services generate 75 percent of revenue from total sales.

With the purchase of the Jaguar Land Rover brand, Tata has made a significant presence in the luxury car market.

He has introduced a new dimension of his skill and vision by building the world's lowest priced car. He is also looking towards American aeronautics in the future and has tied up with the American company Sikorsky to set up a helicopter manufacturing factory in Hyderabad.

Ratan Tata wants Tata companies to prove that they can compete with companies in developed countries and stay steadfast in emerging markets.

Along with this, they are also discharging social responsibilities with utmost preparedness. Tata group is also devoted to public welfare work. Ratan Tata is doing this through his various trusts. These charitable trusts hold about 66 percent of Tata Sons' shares. Tata entered into the retail, telecom, biotech and other sectors by involving the marginal business companies, which focused on the cosmetics, paints and cement business and made a strong footprint in many areas.

Today the Tata Group has around 100 companies and 300 ancillaries, which trade in 40 businesses. The group is threaded together through limited employees of the holding company—Tata Sons and Tata Industries. Both these holding companies work under the chairmanship of Ratan Tata. These two companies only work as controller of strategic vision and Tata based and help in big agreements. Bombay House, a group corporate office set up by Ratan Tata, also leaves its mark on these companies. The nine senior executives of Tata companies are members of the board of the Tata company, which discharges corporate responsibility. Ratan Tata participates in major agreements as chief executive.

Ratan Tata's role in the Corus Agreement was pioneering. This was an ambitious level of work and the amount of money involved was also very substantial. Yet Ratan Tata persevered unwaveringly. He had faith in himself and his group.

The Tata Steel Company spends millions of rupees annually on about 800 villages around the site of the establishment, which are spent on projects such as education, health and agricultural development.

Jamshedpur, established in 1908, is home to about 7,00,000 people today, with a Tata workforce of around 20,000. Despite this, Tata Steel has carried the responsibility of all public facilities and schools in the city.

Ratan Tata has a calm disposition. Always away from publicity, he does his work silently without attracting the attention of people. He buys companies and brands around the world. In this way, he has transformed a family group into a multinational company today. In July 2009, when US Secretary of State Hillary Clinton came to India, she expressed her condolences to the victims of the 26/11 terrorist attacks in a booklet of condolences kept there. In the Taj Hotel itself, she discussed matters of mutual interest with selected Indian industrialists and some important personalities of the business world. Ratan Tata hosted this meeting.

❑

Something More About Ratan Tata

Who can forget the 26/11 terror attack in Mumbai, when ten terrorists crossed the Indian maritime border into Mumbai and fired indiscriminately at several places and killed many people? But many people may not know what the Tata group did for its employees affected by the attack.

The Tata group considered all categories of employees, including those working as temporary employees for day, on duty while the hotel was closed.

Employees' salaries were sent by money order during the hotel closure. Not only this, a psychiatric unit was also established to provide counselling facilities to the needy in collaboration with the Tata Institute of Social Sciences. A mentor was assigned to each employee and it was the responsibility of the person to act as a 'single window clearance' for all the help the employee sought. Ratan Tata himself met the families of 80 employees injured or dead in this attack. He asked these family members and dependents what kind of help they expected from him.

In a record time of twenty days, the Tata group formed a trust aimed at helping employees. The unique thing in this was that other people affected by the attack, such as railway employees, police personnel, people walking on the pavement, who had no connection with the Tatas, were also brought under compensation. During this attack, many vendors who lost their means of livelihood were provided with hand carts by Tata.

All senior managers, including Ratan Tata, were busy in the last visit (*antim yatra*) of the dead for three consecutive days. It was a really terrible phase. The provided facilities mentioned below, in terms of each of its deceased employees by Tata costed in the range from ₹ 36 to 85 lakh.

1. The lifetime amount equal to the last salary of the employee to family and dependents.
2. To take full responsibility for the education of dependents and children anywhere in the world.
3. Lifetime medical care to the whole family and dependents.
4. All debts and advance payments are forgiven—no matter how substantial the amount.
5. Lifelong counselling facility for every person.

Mantra is that if you care about your employees then the employees will also give their life for your product. Companies thinking of employee interest never have to face a problem like holding them back.

(Sincerely: N. Raghuraman, '*Dainik Bhaskar*')

References

1. www.tata.com
2. www.srtt.org
3. www.tatamotors.com
4. www.businessworld.in
5. www.deshgujarat.com
6. www.daylife.com
7. www.team-bhp.com
8. www.livemint.com
9. www.photogallery.outlookindia.com
10. www.pmindia.nic.in
11. www.thesagefoundation.com

❑

Success Secrets

Author's Note

The general notion of history teaches us that the success graph of a kingdom rises higher and after reaching a climax point, the glory tumbles down headlong. When an empire begins to be built, it becomes quite evident for the establisher to suggest innovative ideas and some ideologically superlative perspectives that can set a new throne up and strengthen it. But the continuation of the glory depends how the successors carry forward the legacy and maintain the balance right from the beginning. Though "Adversity always presents opportunities for introspection", some sort of dismissal happens from the hierarchical end, and the entire apartment is gradually shattered. If we look at the Mughal Empire, Babur established it with his highest power; Akbar carried forward the legacy successfully. But then the empire declined from several corners and points, and finally was destroyed in the long run.

But the exception of Tatas' managing business became quite a trademark in Indian history as it successfully carried forward the lineage without hampering the focused aim, though variably differed in different sectors. But from the days of Jamsetji Tata up to now, the Tatas consistently worked hard, thought and re-thought the process of making business superfluous with moderate improvisation and important modification. As history progresses, different 'leaders' appear and lead the monopoly with heavy responsibilities, thus strengthening the dynasty.

Ratan Tata is finally the one to be discussed and well-talked because of his amazing quality of understanding the public impulse, along with the contemporary societal study and political influence. He never failed to justify his forerunners perfectly, even when at the time of crisis, but dealt with every affair successfully, made their business to spread all over, and simultaneously opening some innovative corridors of ideas for the youth of India.

– Vinod Sharma

❑

When the Baton Decides to Shift

It is back to one fine morning of 1991. The 87-year-old J.R.D. Tata had been the chairman of Tata for more than half a century. With the group's leading companies managed also by geriatric satraps, the last thing the Tata name stood for were flamboyance and energy; the more usual adjectives were staid and unenterprising. That was when a fairly young Ratan Tata (53) was selected as the group's new chairman, provoking questions about his performance (undistinguished) and so that of the capability, almost apart from the acceptability. Though the questions were answered long ago, but as usual, the acceptability was attained only by eliminating out some grey hairs. Two decades later, as a 75-year-old Ratan Tata planned to step down in 2012, the Tata group still stood for vibrancy, energy and enthusiasm to move forward, doing the business in typically the way Tata was known for. The monopoly never ended in Tata with just the absence of any household tycoon, as 44-year-old Cyrus Mistry took charge from then with a promising vibe.

Tatas' working ethics and success principles were based on looking forward always with an innovative as well as daring (especially for the blue-prints overseas) ideas, along with tight shareholding and brand discipline. As Rahul Bajaj correctly remarked, Ratan Tata has changed the DNA – almost entirely for the better.

When India was opening up for globalization, liberalization and privatization in 1991, the iconic Tata group was pioneering a major organizational shake-up in terms of installing a non-committal Ratan Tata as successor of J.R.D. Tata. Indeed the top operation platoon working nearly with J.R.D. Tata had no indication about the transition. Also, Ratan Tata had no success stories that could inspire his elderly associates to accept him as the new chairman of the Tata Group. Still, no one had the guts to question the wisdom of J.R.D. Tata and therefore began the Ratan Tata period in the Tata Group.

The preliminary challenge for Ratan Tata was to establish his authority and increase effectiveness across the group companies which largely worked singly. For long, the Tata group companies had worked in a decentralized mode. But the decentralized arrangement deteriorated under the competitive forces that knocked at the doors of the country in the wake of opening up of the Indian economy at the decree of the International Monetary Fund and the World Bank. There could not have been a better and more intriguing time to take charge of the Tata Group for Ratan Tata "Who was at the right place at the right time and could see what was happening around him and respond accordingly". (Datta, 2012).

The group always finds options for amplifying its range, as it was 18 times bigger already than that of its width in 1991, if counted in US dollars; in rupees, it is 51 times bigger, and competed against successful tug-of-war with the rest of the corporate houses in India, dominating with highest appliance. The growth figures for gains are also fascinating. Both have been helped by the astral performance of Tata

Consultancy Services (TCS), which remains the country's largest software services establishment. TCS also subsidized much of the increased intra-group shareholding and asset accession drives. But indeed without TCS, the group's performance under Ratan Tata has been phenomenal. Though growth in market capitalization (without TCS, which was listed only in 2004) has been below par at an annual rate of 10.8 per cent. The return on capital employed too has declined, from 15.2 per cent in 1992 to 14.4 per cent indeed with TCS — reflecting the below-rated performance of some of the overseas means, and the fact that an on-again-off-again Tata Motors has by far the smallest price-earnings multiple in the vehicle industry.

It is also important to note the particular quality with which Ratan Tata has conducted himself throughout these two dynamic and frequently tumultuous decades, and to admit that he long ago became the doyen of Indian industry. Sophisticatedly dressed, and moving calmly and quietly among the world's business tycoons, Mr. Tata has also acquired global standing for himself and his group — becoming, with ease, the largest private employer in the UK. Some would question his support of Narendra Modi when the Tata Nano project moved to Gujarat, others would point to the reproach at Tata Finance (led at the time by someone who had worked with Mr. Tata), and many will keep in mind Niira Radia and her formidable attempts to blow the choice of telecom minister in 2009. Mr. Tata has also had his run-sways with the media, repetitively denying words attributed to him, being most sensitive about criticism, and blacklisting one large media house after the other when it came to group advertising. But these are minor aspects of an impressive business career that in the end has more than justified J.R.D.'s choice of successor in 1991, and which leaves the Tata name shining brighter than the others.

❑

How the Legacy Continued to Rule

The Tata Group appeared in the scenario when Jamsetji Nusserwanji Tata started a trading establishment in 1868. The group set foot into manufacturing in 1874 (fabrics) and into services in 1904 (Hotels). Jamsetji's planning to advocate and set up new industries in the country was sustained by his son, Sir Dorabji Tata who succeeded him as the chairman of the group. He set up India's first steel factory in 1907, its first cement manufacturing unit in 1912 and the first indigenous insurance company in 1919. Each of these units was set up as an individual company. The Chairman of Tata Sons, the holding company and the chief protagonist of the group traditionally emerged as the Chairman of the Tata group. The members of the board of Tata Sons and Tata Industries, the other investment arms of the Group, are generally also members of the boards of different group companies.

Tata Group had always been avant-garde for the others of the contemporary time. And this pioneering spirit was not only limited to the world of business, but also propagated its zeitgeist to a broader extent. The group set up some of India's prestigious institutions – Indian Institute of Science, Tata Memorial Hospital, Tata Institute of Fundamental Research, Tata Institute of Social Sciences, Tata Energy Research Institute, and National Centre for Performing Arts. Jamsetji Tata said, "We do not claim to be more unselfish, more generous or more philanthropic than other people. But we think we started on sound principles, considering the interests of the shareholders our own, and the health and welfare of the employees, the sure foundation of our successive."

Lord Curzon, the then Viceroy of India, conceded the pioneering contribution of Jamsetji Tata. No other Indian, even today, has done better for the commercial trades and industry of India.

Jamsetji's sons, Sir Dorabji Tata, and Sir Ratanji Tata donated the utmost of their heritage and wealth for the welfare of the society when they established the Sir Dorabji Tata Trust and the Sir Ratan Tata Trust, independently. After Sir Dorabji's unfortunate death in 1932, Sir Nowroji Saklatwala, the third chairman of the group, continued the tradition of charity and donation for public welfare through several trusts. As a result, nearly two-thirds of the shares in Tata Sons are in custody of various charitable trusts. J.R.D. Tata (J.R.D.), who succeeded Saklatwala as the chairman of the group in 1938, explained, "The Tatas are in fact a trust and an institution more than just a business house. Right from the early days I knew Mahatma Gandhi and I was quite impressed and believed in the spirit of trusteeship ... I think that is the best way to apply the spirit of trusteeship – to act as trustees and to consider major problems of the country in connection with the firm as trustees and not as businessmen merely trying to make money for the firm. Incidentally, we want to make money because that is the only way to make funds available to charitable trusts".

JRD joined the Tata group in 1925 upon his father's urging, before he could complete his university education, prompting JRD to say, "Because of a lack of technical knowledge, my main contribution in management was to encourage others."

During the 52 times of JRD's leadership, the group entered varied businesses, growing from 14 companies in 1938 to a 95 company group in 1991, which included some of the flagship companies of the Group in 2016 – Tata Chemicals, Tata Motors, Tata Consultancy Services (TCS), Tata Tea and Titan Industries. While referring to the relationship between Tata Sons and its vividly associated companies, JRD had said, "I would call it a group of individually managed companies united by two factors ... that they are part of a larger group, the Tatas. Each company enjoys its share of privilege. Second, there is innate loyalty, a sharing of certain beliefs."

Over the times, to increase growth, JRD had allowed the dilution of Tata Sons' stake in the group companies performing in the group holding company having only a small, some would say emblematic, stake in the numerous group companies. In 1969, when the Government of India with a view to check the power of large business groups similar to the Tatas, introduced the Monopolies and Restrictive Trade Practices Act, the Tata group claimed that its cells were competently and resourcefully maintained by independent companies and J.R.D. was just a part-time chairman. J.R.D. said, "...Today, except in Tata Sons, I do not wield any kind of executive authority. But because I am senior in age, I operate more on the basis of influence and confidence."

Indeed when the non-supervisory restrictions were eased in the 1980s, J.R.D. Tata did not feel the need to institutionalize the group cooperation. Speaking to Tata group historian, R. M. Lala, J.R.D. elucidated his leadership style, "...with each man I have my own way. I am one who will make full allowance for a man's character and idiosyncrasies. You have to adapt yourself to their ways and deal accordingly and draw out the best in each man. One of the qualities of leadership is to assess what is needed to get the best results for an enterprise. If that demands being a very active executive chairman, as I was in Air India, I did that. On the other hand, in one of our other companies where I know that the managing director wishes to be alone and will get the results that way, it will be stupid for me to come in the way. At times, it involves suppressing yourself. It is painful but necessary ... To lead men; you have to lead them with affection."

Accordingly, CEOs of large Tata enterprises surfaced themselves as independent leaders in the Tata group. Tata experts—similar as—Darbari Seth, who played a crucial part in founding Tata Chemicals and Tata Tea, Ajit Kerkar who was necessary in promoting the Indian Hotels business, Tata Steel chairman Russi Mody, who successfully led the company through tough times, prestigious jurist Nani Palkhivala who was chairman of ACC Ltd. – emerged as important leaders in the Tata group. Kerkar observed, "He was the kind of chairman any professional manager should have. He laid down the policies but in no way interfered with the day-to-day working. ... He never imposed his own will on anything. That was his greatness".

During his term, JRD started group-wide enterprise similar to the Tata Administrative Services (TAS) to groom talented individuals for advanced operation careers in Tata companies, sustained Jamsetji's user-friendly ideologies by initiating various hand best-practices – an eight-hour working day, free medical aid, workers' provident scheme, and workmen's accident compensation schemes – that recently were made into law. For his social and entrepreneurial trials, J.R.D. Tata was awarded, India's loftiest mercenary honour, the Bharat Ratna, in 1992. He was the only businessman to have received the honour.

❑

The New Captain: His Tournaments

Ratan Tata does not need any preface due to his fandom in trade-circles, for the group's achievements and being the most successful industrialist of India. He is popular in the launch-up circles for inspiring the youth through his life, ideology and especially the energy with which he capsized the failure of numerous companies to churn a profit, making the empire dazzlingly successful. The group has had great wealth which eventually has allowed it to grow by leaps and bounds in its continuance. He once commented that rise and fall is necessary in one's career as even the straight line in the ECG curve means lifelessness. He reminds the young generation that, to rise in the long run overcomes the short term failures.

He was born on December 28, 1937, in Surat, to Naval and Sonoo Tata. Naval Tata was the espoused son of Jamsetji Tata and Ratan Tata was raised by his paternal grandmother Lady Navajbai Tata after his parents' separation. Although they remained in contact, Ratan could not get the love, indulgence, support or the guidance from his own parents. He was close to his grandmother, who looked after him and raised him. She was a strict woman with a well-regulated approach to life and tasks.

Ratan Tata studied armature at Cornell University in the United States of America and had a job offer from IBM. Ratan Tata recollected, "I was quite happy with my work and, given a choice, I would have remained in the US". Still, he had to return to India in 1962, when Lady Navajbai's health deteriorated. Upon JRD's assignation, Ratan Tata joined the group and began his career 1962 as apprentice at the Jamshedpur factory of Tata Steel Ltd., also known as Tata Iron and Steel Company (TISCO). Over the coming 10 years, prior to being given the responsibility of turning around the ailing NELCO, Ratan Tata had stints in different group companies. Once, NELCO, one of the largest manufacturers of radios in the country, had lower than 3 per cent market shares and had significant accumulated losses when Ratan Tata took charge. Over the coming three years under his captainship, NELCO recovered achieving a market share of 20 per cent and taking back or retrieving its losses. Still in 1977, even though Ratan Tata believed in the abecedarian soundness of NELCO, the company was closed down owing to problems with the workers' union.

Soon after, Ratan Tata was given the responsibility to turn around Mumbai-grounded Empress Mills, yet another ailing company in the group. But his plans to contemporize the company did not receive the blessing of Tata Sons. He managed to energize the workers, but could not get acceptable backing support from the top management of Tata Group. Workers' strike worsened the script and eventually the Empress Mill was closed in 1986. Ratan Tata said, "At around this time, the whole Indian textile industry went through a bad patch. So, some Tata directors, chiefly Nani Palkhivala, took the line that we should liquidate the mill. I argued with them. We demanded just ₹50 lakhs (5 million) to turn it around. But Nani opposed giving us the money and we closed the mill down".

The experience with NELCO and Empress nudged Ratan Tata, a member of the panel of Tata Sons since 1974, to write to J.R.D. Tata about the need to have a strategic plan for the group, "I am strongly advocating the initiation of such a plan by the chairman as I personally see signs of our disintegration as a group. The first issue that needs to be addressed is whether we, as Tatas, see ourselves operating in the next 5 to 10 years as a single unified group, or a loosely connected agglomeration of independent companies ... If at all it is decided that the Tatas should operate as a group, then several strategic decisions need to be taken relating to the projected organizational and operational structure of the Tatas." Ratan Tata recalled, "I used to discuss the matter with JRD, why don't we find a mechanism to pull ourselves together? At that time, I was looking at a logo – not the new one – and was asking why don't we use that as glue and demand things from companies and give things to companies. But he never really supported that because he felt that it was not necessary. And from his standpoint, he was the patriarch, they were his team and there was no need to do all this."

In 1983, soon after he was appointed the chairman of Tata Industries, Ratan Tata progressed with a group-wide strategic plan, which proposed the invention of the newest technology supports, adding the group's transnational business and moving out of underperforming businesses. The plan also suggested that the group companies cash in on the group's size and variety and stressed making Tata a more unified structure through increased power. Tata Industries, which after the rescinding of the managing agency system had been without a clear accreditation, came as the group's vehicle for entry into the proposed new businesses. Fresh equity infusion from group companies – Tata Steel, Tata Motors, Indian Hotels Co., Tata Oil Mills Co., Tata Chemicals, and Voltas – evolved in Tata Industries pursuing several of the recently linked openings.

More recently, following his appointment as Chairman of Tata Motors, Ratan Tata encouraged the company to expand its portfolio. Tata Motors first entered the mileage vehicles segment with the launch of Tata Sumo and followed it up by entering into a common adventure with Mercedes Benz to assemble cars for trade in India and explore the capability for exports.

Ratan Tata's engagement as chairman of the group coincided with the liberalization of the Indian economy, which radically changed India's commercial topography. The steering in of global competition urged several people to prognosticate that Indian companies after having operated in a secured economy for decades would lose out to new and nimble competition. The Tata group was considered particularly vulnerable due to its size, diversity, decentralized structure, and therefore the recent retirement of its long serving chairman, J.R.D. Tata. Ratan Tata agreed saying, "I think the group needed cohesion, or let me put that another way, the cohesion the group had was through the persona of J.R.D. Tata, the patriarch. My concern was that after him, it would be difficult to hold it together."

❑

The Tycoon Typhoon

In the 1980s when JRD started considering his choice of the next heir, interposers at the Tata group thought that Russi Mody would succeed him. Ratan Tata said, "For most of the 1980s, I personally thought that Russi was certain to be the next head of Tatas. He ran Tata Steel very successfully, had a larger-than-life personality and Jeh (JRD) was very fond of him. Russi was gregarious. He was outgoing. He could go into a crowd of workers and charm them."

In 1988, JRD asked Russi Mody to also head Tata Motors. Still, when Russi Mody spoke disparagingly about Tata Motors to the press, the also Tata Motors' chairman, Sumant Moolgaonkar refused to hand over charge to Mody and sought the appointment of Ratan Tata as the company's chairman. Later, in March 1991, when JRD declared the comparatively less known and reticent Ratan Tata as his successor, it caused unusual drama and displeasure within the group. Unlike the opposite contenders for the position, Ratan Tata had no displayable success till even the two Tata companies that he headed ahead, NELCO and Empress Mills had folded up. Remembering his initial days, Ratan

Tata stated, "J.R.D. Tata had around him a team of senior managers, all of them people of substantial understanding in their respective spheres. While they may have acceded to his wish that I take over the chairmanship – and this happened suddenly – I must confess that I did not feel any sense of joyousness on their part, because some of them had aspirations to have the job themselves."

Ratan Tata's concerns about the group's outlook stemmed to some extent from the structural tribulations that he encountered as a chairman. He had little control over the companies because of the low ownership stakes that Tata Sons held in them. Also, during the 53 years of JRD's tenure of chairmanship, the chieftains of group companies had total freedom with little authorial countersign and that they made it clear that they wished to protect their respective fields. Darbari Seth, Chairman of Tata Chemicals and Tata Tea, put it bluntly, "The Tata group is a commonwealth of enterprises, not an empire".

Ratan Tata had his first battle with Russi Mody when the second appointed Aditya Kashyap, his protégé, as joint managing director, without the permission of the company's board. Only after JRD's intervention and multiple conversations with the board did Mody withdraw his decision.

The two got further in moral combat when in early 1992 Ratan Tata revived an old policy that set the retirement age for administrative directors (including managing directors and executive chairmen) at 65 years and for non-executive directors at 75 years. Mody, 74 years at that time, complied by giving up his administrative position and continued as the non-executive chairman of Tata Steel. Still, before he was to retire fully from Tata Steel, his conflict with the Tata Steel board and Ratan Tata boosted, frequently in the public sphere. An agonized Ratan Tata said, "I don't understand why Russi behaved the way he did. He was my friend. He was Jeh's favourite. But he just became totally unreasonable. I remember one board meeting where we asked him why he kept giving interviews running down Tata Steel, of which he was the chairman. (J.J. Irani was MD.) He just got up and said, 'I will leave the room because this subject has been raised.' And then, to our astonishment, the chairman of Tata Steel got up and walked out of his own board meeting. After that he didn't turn up for board meetings and kept maligning the company. Finally, the board had to remove him."

The unfortunate competitiveness of the two flagship companies of the group Tata Steel and Tata Motors, of which he was now the chairman, was the second most important challenge for Ratan Tata. Years of leadership, achieved in an unrestricted frugality isolated from serious competition, had rendered these companies with an organizational culture that had scant regard for cost, quality, or client satisfaction. Presumably in the changed environment, both the companies, which constituted 50 per cent of the group's development, faced a severe decline in their earnings and profits in 1992. Ratan Tata set about transubstantiating them. He said, "I made no effort to play a group part until TISCO and TELCO were doing extremely well."

Apart from concentrating on the three crucial motorists of competitiveness, he made significant investments in upgrading their technology and revamping their product portfolio. While Tata Steel increased the share of value-added products in its client immolations, Tata Motors blazoned its plans to produce an indigenously developed passenger car, Indica. Still, the company's plans to incursion into passenger cars met with dubitation. Judges considered the move veritably parlous as the company, basically a manufacturer of marketable vehicles, had no experience in designing cars. The venture if it failed could ruin the company. Ratan Tata did not agree, "I think risk is a necessary part of business philosophy. You can be risk-averse and take no risks, in which case you will have a certain trajectory in terms of your growth. Or you can, while being prudent, take a greater risk in order to grow faster. I think, as a group, we were risk-averse and we hardly grew because either it was not safe or no one else had done it ahead. I view risk as an ability to be where no one has been before. I view risk to be an issue of thinking big, something we did not do previously. We did everything in small increments so we always lagged behind."

Over the next two years, the advancements in quality and productivity resulted in both companies' recording significant advancements in their performance. Indeed, while helping the flagship companies ameliorate performance, in order to grab the new openings made available by profitable reforms, Ratan Tata entered into collaborations with multinationals and set up several high technology foundations such as Tata Teleservices (Bell Canada) and Tata Communications in the telecom sector, Tata Petrodyne in upstream oil and gas (with BP), Tata Information Systems in information technology (with IBM) and initiated conversations with Singapore Airlines to launch airline services in India. To fund the new initiatives, Ratan Tata vended 20 per cent stakes in Tata Industries Ltd. to the Hong Kong grounded Jardine Matheson group for $35 million (Rs. 1.26 billion).

As a primary step towards integrating and getting the different cells to favour support a group, Ratan Tata sought to extend Tata Sons' stake within the group companies. Tata Sons made a rights issue of equity shares for ₹3 billion and the different trusts renounced their rights in favour of the group companies who subscribed to the equity. The fund therefore raised was used to increase the stake in group companies. Ratan Tata explained, "There was a question whether we had the right to claim to manage these companies. In fact we didn't have the legal right, or even the moral right, to manage them. Then we set ourselves the task of seeing how we could put ourselves together as a more meaningful and recognizable group of companies with more central control."

Organizing the different businesses into a coherent structure came next. With the help of the consulting establishment, McKinsey & Company, Ratan Tata organized the various businesses into seven sectors — information technology and communications, engineering products and services, accoutrements, services, energy, consumer products, and chemicals. Many of the cells had overlapping businesses—ACC, Tata Chemicals, and TISCO made cement; Merind and Tata Pharma had presence in the medicinal field. These businesses were moreover consolidated into one of the cells or vended. Ratan Tata elaborated, "The kind of structural change that we are seeking is giving more attention to performance and measurement of performance, greater mobility between companies in terms of manpower and a greater focus in companies on strategic issues rather than on tactical operations."

Along with the reformation, Ratan Tata started enterprises to strengthen the group's cohesion. In 1998, he introduced the Tata Brand Equity and Business Promotion Agreement between Tata Sons and the group companies. The agreement quested that Tata Sons, the proprietor of the Tata name and brand totem, would promote the group brand and cover the interests of the group companies, both in India and worldwide. The Tata brand name itself was to be worn with significant concern. If an undertaking company fell outside the core businesses of the group or was perceived as a parlous new adventure where the group had limited experience, the Tata name was not used. One such company was Trent, the retail venture, started by Simone Tata, following the trade of Lakme to the Unilever subsidiary in India, Hindustan Unilever.

Though the agreement was not obligatory, companies that wanted to use the Tata name were needed to take part in the programme by paying an annual figure to Tata Sons. The Tata Brand Equity agreement divided the companies into two categories – companies that used the Tata name directly, and had a strong association with the Tata name; and companies that did not use the Tata name directly. With an intention to produce single strong equity that would profit all the companies, it was proposed that the first tier companies would contribute 0.25 per cent of development, or 5 per cent of profit before duty, whichever was less. Further, the other pealed companies would contribute 0.15 per cent of the development. Ratan Tata said, "If you are to fight a Mitsubishi or an X or Y in the free India of tomorrow, you better have one rather than 40 brands. You better have the ability to promote that brand in a meaningful manner."

The tax of brand figure was explosively blamed by the old bureaucrats and critics. Nani Palkhivala, the then chairman of ACC, affirmed that while ACC was an associate of the group, it was not a Tata Group company. Ajit Kerkar, chairman and managing director of Indian Hotels argued the company had no way used the Tata name and hence did not owe a figure to Tata Sons. Echoing these sentiments, the well-known columnist Swaminathan Aiyar wrote, "So many Tata branded products have flopped that the Tata brand is by no means a winner. The group's textile mills and Tata Oil fell sick; Lakme was sold before it suffered a similar fate. Titan Watches and Indian Hotels have prospered but neither carries the Tata name ... TISCO and TELCO have created the Tata reputation and cynics will say they should demand money from Ratan Tata for giving his name similar prestige and not the other way around."

Ratan Tata in defence observed "When a company would go to its bankers, it was part of the Tata group; when it went to seek a new collaboration, the literature spent a long time talking about the Tata group of which it was a part. But, after those situations that had been achieved the issue of being a member of the Tata group sort of slipped into a lower grade."

Signatories to the brand contract were needed to pledge the Tata Code of Conduct that codified the group's translucent and moral business practices. They also demanded to meet with certain performance conditions, which included being among the top three in their separate industries, double their turnover every four years and, profit after tax every three years. Ratan Tata said, "Over the years we didn't standard ourselves against the best of the breed, either in India or globally. Some companies never looked at market share, and we always compared ourselves traditionally to our past ... many of them got into the phase of reacting to the market rather than being proactive."

In December 1998, seven of the Tata companies—TISCO, TELCO, Tata Tea, Tata Chemicals, the Tata Electric Companies, Tata International, and Tata Industries—signed the agreement. To make the Tata name more prominent and suggestive of the Tata connection to its companies in the minds of the stakeholders, TISCO was renamed as Tata Steel and TELCO appeared as Tata Motors. The different ensigns used by group companies were also replaced with a common group totem.

To help him oversee the restructuring sweats, Ratan Tata found a five-member group administrative office (GEO). The members were N.A. Soonawala, Director of Tata Sons, R. Gopalakrishnan (Executive Director, Tata Sons), Ishaat Hussain (Executive Director, Finance, TISCO and later, Director, Finance, Tata Sons), Kishore Chaukar (Managing Director, Tata Industries Limited) and Manab Bose (Director, Human Resources, Tata Group). The GEO was a companion to group companies in strategic planning, benchmarking performance, and in allocating assets. To oversee performance and to enhance the commerce between the superintendents of the affiliated companies and Tata Sons, the GEO set up Business Review Panels (BRC) for each of the cells. The panels comported of representatives from Tata Sons and external agencies such as financial institutions. Ratan Tata noted "The BRC is not focusing on what is necessary for the Tata group ... It is not an internal Tata board, it is a committee of the company's board ... The BRC focuses on trying to make a company more profitable, more productive ... In fact, the directors of the companies were concerned that this would take away the autonomy of the board. It is not so. The BRC will, in fact, eventually make its recommendation to the board through this board committee and the board will finally take its decision."

To help companies identify areas of betterment, the Tata Business Excellence Model (TBEM) was introduced. The TBEM, which was modeled along the lines of the Malcolm Balridge National Quality Award, set a brand for all Tata companies all through seven core aspects of business operations: leadership, strategic planning, client focus, dimension, analysis and knowledge operation, workforce focus, process operation and issues of fiscal and non-financial parameters, and business results. The JRD Quality Value award was to be given to the company that scored the highest on the benchmarking.

Tata Motors launched Indica which got rave reviews for its design and comfort. Still soon, client complaints about the product quality and machine performance started coming in. Deals did not go as anticipated. Tata Motors reported a net loss of ₹5 billion because of the commuter auto blueprint, the biggest loss posted by any private sector company in India and the highest loss in the history of the Tata group. The company improved its gains by following the TBEM recommendations of quality enhancement, cost reduction, re-engineering of processes, and new product development. Also, Tata Steel embraced TBEM recommendations to come out as one of the smallest cost manufacturers of steel in the world and aligned its product processes to market dynamics. The company brought down its per-ton cost of product from $225 to $150, the second lowest worldwide. B Muthuraman, Managing Director, Tata Steel, asserted, "With all these sweats, Tata Steel, by the year 2001, had become one of the lowest cost producers of steel in the world and began to be recognized in the global steel industry. We had earned the right to grow."

In 2002, Ratan Tata founded the Group Corporate Centre (GCC), initially consisted of himself and other senior group executives – N.A. Soonawala, R.K. Krishna Kumar and J.J. Irani - to give premeditated track and escalation openings to the group companies and made the GEO its managerial arm. To patron the expansion of the group, Tata Sons made TCS public. The group vended 13 stakes in the company for $1.2 billion (Rs. 54.2 billion). Ratan Tata said, "The proceeds from the IPO will be used to help the Tata group continue restructuring its balance sheet, promoting new ventures, and deepening its involvement in existing group companies."

Companies responded to Ratan Tata's call for promoting new initiatives by bearing several new systems. In the marketable vehicle section, Tata Motors could relate the need for a four-wheeled vehicle that could serve as a last-afar distribution transport. For ferrying goods over small distances there were either exchanges, which were expensive or there were three-wheeled auto cabs that were unsafe and energy hamstrung. The company launched Tata Ace in 2005 that was priced on par with three-wheeler auto-rickshaws but had the cargo capacities of a four-wheeler truck and importantly, handled safety and maneuverability suitable to Indian roads. The product was a moment megahit.

In the new technology areas, the group established presence altogether aspects of telecom services – land-line and wireless services employing CDMA technology through Tata Telecom, GSM cellular services through collaboration with AT&T and Birlas, long distance calling, internet and value-added services through Tata Communications, following the accession of state-possessed company Videsh Sanchar Nigam Limited.

In the technology business, with a view to globalize its footmark, Tata Tea sought to acquire Tetley, the UK-grounded global tea major. The company's $318 million shot failed as it could not put together its backing arrangements well in time. R.K. Krishna Kumar, Managing Director of Tata Tea at that time recalled, "We realized that we had to get our act together on our funding arrangements well in advance, if we ever desired to make such a large global acquisition. It was a lesson well learnt."

In 2000, when Tetley came up for trade again, Tata Tea bid $435 million and won. The preemption was the group's first transnational accession and the largest cross-border preemption by an Indian company at that time. Tata Tea, which was a third of the size of Tetley beat competition from US consumer products major Sara Lee and Nestle, the Swiss foods major and surfaced as the world's second largest tea company with deals in 44 countries. Ratan Tata affirmed,

"In a world where brand strength is crucial, the acquisition of Tetley will give Tata Tea a global opportunity."

The deal was substantially financed through a debt of $320 million, and as a consequence, Tetley continued to function as an "independent" company with Tata Tea playing largely a monitoring part. Homi Khusrokhan, the then managing director of Tata Tea, said, "A leveraged buy-out has perforce certain limitations attached to it, in terms of what you can and can't do as long as the high leverage continues. Therefore, in the early days following the acquisition, Tata Tea restricted its role to an advisory one: monitoring, guiding and watching over Tetley's operations."

After two years, Tata Tea and Tata Sons raised their stake in the company, released high cost debt, and integrated Tetley's operations to capture solidarity in areas of tea buying and blending.

The Tetley accession was the launch of the globalization drive at the Tata Group. The Group Centre signed Alan Rosling from Jardine Matheson to forefront the operation and Arun Gandhi, a leading chartered accountant, who had advised Tata Tea in the Tetley accession to give the necessary valuation and taxation moxie. Ratan Tata said, "I have felt for some time that we have been an inward looking group. We could have gone overseas much earlier; the Aditya Birla Group did that many years ago. But we were obsessed with ourselves in India. And I suddenly felt – certainly when I started to sit on boards overseas — very conspicuous by the fact that we were only in India".

Over the coming decade, the Tata Group companies made a string of accessions. Affiliated companies linked targets that either filled gaps in their product portfolios or handed sourcing advantages or gave access to new geographical markets. The GCC handed M&A premonitory support, helped the group companies to unite capital, assessed whether the target company would fit into the Tata's values and handed post-acquisition integration support. Importantly, it acted as a repository of knowledge and moxie transferring literacy from former accessions to the affiliated cells. Speaking of its accession of Daewoo Commercial Vehicle Company in Korea, Ravi Kant, and Vice Chairman of Tata Motors said, "Tata Motors was one of ten bidders, including Chinese and European companies. Initially, we faced some difficulty in being accepted as a serious bidder. I think the one thing that helped us win the deal was our philosophy. Mr. Ratan Tata suggested that we should see ourselves as a Korean company, not as an Indian company in Korea. That made all the difference."

In the starting quarter of 2007, Tata Motors acquired the ailing decoration luxury car brand Jaguar and top of the line mileage vehicle brand Land Rover from Ford Motor Company for roughly $2.3 billion. Though Tata Motors intended to buy only the Land Rover, Ford was selling both the brands (JLR) as a combo. The GCC helped Tata Motors raise the $3 billion (about ₹120 billion) from multiple banks. Critics and investors said Tata Motors was making a huge mistake, especially since experienced car makers similar to BMW and Ford could not turn around JLR. Still, Ratan Tata saw it as a unique occasion to move into prime section with access to world class iconic brands. Ravi Kant said, "The deal has dramatically changed the perception of Tata Motors worldwide. People see us differently now, with greater respect. Doors that were closed earlier are now opening. People are coming on their own from all corners of the world and making so many offers. It created a great impact."

The economic crisis occurred soon after the deal closed, and demand for luxury cars tumbled in Europe and North America — its two biggest markets. Tata Motors posted a loss of $520 million in financial year 2009. Analysts were not so astonished; they were rather out in droves with their "we told you so" reports. Undeterred, the company indeed as it embarked on a serious cost reduction action, explored new market deals in other countries, like China, Saudi Arabia, Russia, etc. By 2010, JLR turned profitable and soon came the dependence of Tata Motors in terms of both earnings and gains.

Still, JLR was not Tata group's biggest accession to date. Towards the end of 2006, Tata Steel acquired British Steel maker, Corus for $12.1 billion, following a competitive bidding process. Tata Steel had gained experience in acquiring Natsteel in Singapore and Millennium Steel in Thailand that strengthened its resource chain and handed access to East Asian markets. The company had originally bid $7.6 billion for Corus, which was challenged by CSN, a Brazilian steel company. The ensuing months observe extreme negotiations from both sides of the deal. Eventually, in January 2007, Tata Steel bought a 100 per cent stake in the Corus. The deal, by far the largest overseas attainment any Indian company made Tata Steel the world's fifth-largest steel patron, with an annual aptitude of 25 million tons.

As in the case of JLR, the 2008 recession deeply impacted Corus. Several changes in the top operation circuit, slow amalgamation of the company by Tata Steel compounded the challenges and as a result, Corus, a profit-making company at the time of its succession, went astray by $303 million in 2010. While the company managed to turn around the very coming year, following job cuts and asset trade, the debt-laden company was still floundering to ameliorate the performance of its European operations.

While the Tata companies were making rapid strides in international markets with accessions, near home they were developing affordable products that served the lower income zones. Ratan Tata said, "All along, the focus of entrepreneurs and corporations has been to develop products for the top of the pyramid that has about 250-300 million people. Though these people constitute about 25-30 per cent of the population, the need of the hour is to create products and services for the remaining 1.2 billion Indians."

One of the successful inventions from the Tata group was Tata Swach, the world's cheapest water cleaner. Access to clean drinking water has been hectic in most Indian villages, small towns, and semi-urban locales and in matrices of civic areas. Tata group set out to find a market-based result to give clean drinking water and reduce health problems arising from drinking polluted water. As a result of collaboration among TCS, Tata Chemicals and Titan Industries, the Swach technology combined low-cost constituents such as rice cocoon ash with superior nanotechnology. It does not need electricity or running water to operate and meets international water sanctification norms. Its affordable price – ₹500, ₹750 and ₹1000 for three variants – put the product within the reach of consumers at the bottom of the social class.

As chairman of the Tata Group, Ratan Tata concentrated on accelerating functional effectiveness and culture of invention which was all the more important in the wake of increased competitiveness in the country, rising foreign direct investments in nearly all the sectors and changing prospects of the stakeholders. Interventions at the decree of Ratan Tata enabled Tata Steel Ltd. to become the smallest cost steel makers of the world (Datta, 2012). Likewise, significant advancements were witnessed in Tata Motors Ltd. as well.

Ratan Tata strictly strengthened the authority of Tata Sons Ltd. – The holding company of all the Tata Group companies by adding the stakes. Before, Tata Sons Ltd. had non-age stakes in most of the Group companies which made them vulnerable to hostile appropriations. Also, he introduced the system of gross payment by the Group companies for using the Tata brand name. This enhanced the brand equity of Tata Group presently.

Some of the less profitable businesses such as cement, fabrics and cosmetics under the marquee of Tata Group were dropped under the leadership of Ratan Tata. On the other hand, he entered the rising areas such as software, telecommunication, finance and retail. Either, Ratan Tata's major benefactions would include global accessions similar to Tetley Tea, Corus Group, and Jaguar Land Rover.

Ratan Tata is credited with massive financial success during his term as Chairman of the Group. The Group's total deals at the end of 2011-12, at ₹4.51 trillion, was 43 times the development in 1992-93, the first full financial achievement after Tata took over as chairman; while net profit growth in the same period was indeed more spectacular, rising 51 times (Datta, 2012). Also, the entire market capitalization of the group at ₹4.54 trillion in financial years of 2012-13 is 33 times superior than it had been in 1992-93. In the same period, the Sensex, the standard equity indicator of BSE, grew nearly eight times' (Datta, 2012). Still, one of the most precious failures of the Tata Group was Tata Nano – a public car that Ratan Tata promoted despite resistance from within the group.

The Tata Nano was the extreme major action accepted by the group following the observation of Ratan Tata that Indian families that could not enjoy a car demanded a safe and affordable four-wheeler transport. In 2003 at the Geneva Auto Show, Ratan Tata blazoned that the company would develop a people's car that would be priced at $2500. The advertisement attracted transnational attention and the ultra-low-cost car ingrained Nano appeared as the most talked-about car, as world over, people waited for its release. The excitement still did not result in deals when the car was launched in 2009. Ratan Tata said, "The Nano is something I would love to make successful because I don't suppose it has exploited its full potential right now. There has to be another push to make Nano what it can be."

Tata Group Innovation Forum (TGIF) was set up to promote invention. To increase exchange of ideas and learning, TGIF operated a platform, Innoverse, which enabled members to seek results to new problems. Further, to fete the invention efforts of the different group companies, TGIF organized a yearly invention competition entitled - Innovista.

❑

TCS and Tata: The Bosom Friend

Apart from his vision, what helped Ratan Tata pursue his global dreams was the extraordinary success of Tata Consultancy Services, which are 74 per cent possessed by Tata Sons. Beginning with its preliminary public immolation in August 2004, which helped Tata Sons rise to around 2,800 crores; TCS laterally funded the bulk of investments by Tata Sons in major group companies as they sought to conquer the worldwide business of technological matrix. The figures speak for themselves. Since 2004, Tata Sons has invested a bulk amount of ₹34,000 crores in different group companies, including unrecorded gambles. During the period, Tata Sons earned nearly ₹10,000 as dividend from TCS; another ₹9100 crores was raised by dealing TCS shares (including IPO). Again, ₹11,500 crores came from borrowings essentially secured by pledging shares of TCS, the group's most precious company.

So, if not for TCS, Tata might have had to either gauge down his global intentions or the backing cost of big-ticket global accessions would have stretched the group's balance sheet to an unsustainable situations. Investment bankers agree. "The majority control of TCS gives great financial firepower to Tata Sons. The recurring cash from TCS and the market value of TCS provided Tata Sons the cushion to absorb minor losses if the bet didn't work out in the short term," said, Dara Kalyaniwal, vice-president, investment banking, at Prabhudas Lilladher. He is not exaggerating. Tata Sons' wager in TCS is currently valued at around ₹1.8 lakh crores, almost six per cent of which was pledged at the end of September. In comparison, Tata Sons' holding in all listed group companies is presently valued at around Rs 2.4 lakh crores.

TCS has a policy to distribute 30-50 per cent of net profit as dividends, in four quarterly transactions. In FY 2010, still, it distributed 55 per cent of consolidated net profit and 70 per cent of its standalone net profit as equity dividend, by way of a special dividend. Ratings agencies honour the power of TCS, which, they say, plays a significant part in Tata Sons getting overwhelming AAA ratings, helping it to adopt at the smallest possible rate of interest. "The ratings reflect Tata Sons' exceptional financial flexibility which arises from its ability to raise additional funds by sell or pledge of TCS shares," said CRISIL, while assigning top standing to Tata Sons' non-convertible debenture programme in November.

Icra holds an analogous view. "AAA ratings incorporate Tata Sons' strong financial flexibility despite increase in the debt levels to support the funding requirement of its investee companies," said the agency.

The group's globalization drive and its craving for inorganic growth have nearly followed the augmentation of TCS within the last ten years. And, as TCS got larger, so did the aspiration of its chairman. The holding company has dashingly leveraged the newer cash overflows from TCS (as dividends) to adopt and support different group growth plans.

A harmonious fiscal performance by TCS and its high market valuation enabled Tata Sons to act as the investor and lender of last resort to group companies. For instance, when Tata Motors' business rights issue in October 2008 regressed on promoters and Indian Hotels Company's rights issue in 2008 entered muted response from retail and institutional investors. TCS also enabled Tata to see new businesses and nearly half the Tata Sons portfolio is reckoned for by its investment in unrecorded accessories.

As of now, there is no sign of any retardation in the TCS cash machine. In the first half of the FY 2012, net profit rose to 43 per cent, while earnings were over by 36 per cent on a consolidated base. This has restated into handsome earnings for shareholders, including Tata Sons, which has formerly received ₹3,175 crores in the first six months, 30 per cent more than what it earned during the whole of FY 2012. More is waiting to come in the last quarter.

❑

When the Cacophony Sounds Melodious

At a dinner party in Taj Chambers on July 22, 1993, after a lengthy annual general meeting of Tata Steel, Ratan Tata asked B. Muthuraman and T. Mukherjee (elderly general managers then), "Would you let the bluest of blue chip companies have a red bottom line?" The reference of that question was a miserable first quarter result within the background of competition from imports, indicating a transition to a buyer's market. The question helped Tata, who was then new to his post of Tata Steel chairman, prize a pledge from the two gentlemen. Before the end of the financial year, the company would reduce cost by Rs 500 a ton, which restated to 7.5 per cent of the cost at that point in time. Till that time, every year cost had gradually risen.

By December, at a meeting that lasted till two in the morning, Tata was told by a group of veritably satisfied executives that they had managed a cost reduction of ₹350 a ton.

But Tata's reply was a clear sign of dissatisfaction, "Your promise is with me, you don't have to make another promise. What's at stake is your prestige and reputation."

The comment was, thus, loud and clear. By March, costs were reduced by ₹500 a ton indeed, though there was an increase on nearly every other count, including railway freight. Target-led invention had made it possible.

It was an achievement indeed, but towards the late 1990s, profitability started suffering again, urging Tata Steel to appoint three advisers — Booze Allen Hamilton, McKinsey and Arthur D' Little. The report sheet: a grade 'C'.

Tata Steel was told in clear terms that it was inadequate and no good compared to global peers. McKinsey had indeed advised that the steel business was subject to commodity cycles and Tata Steel should diversify.

It came as a rude jolt, but the operation took the cue. From 1995 to 2001, Tata Steel reduced work-power from 78,300 to 47,300 by enforcing a voluntary withdrawal scheme (VRS), and an early separation scheme (ESS). At the administrative position, Tata Steel introduced the performance ethic programme. Had the VRS not been introduced in 1995, all its gains, especially in 2001-02, would have gone towards payment of hires. In a nutshell, Tata Steel would have been in the red.

But the company bounced back. In 2001, it stood first in the World Steel Dynamics (WSD) list of world class steel makers against several parameters that included operating cost, technology, product quality, position in the domestic market.

Small accessions — NatSteel and Millennium Steel— followed and till 2006, that is before Tata Steel acquired Corus, the company featured among the top four steel makers in the world. But following two financial turmoil states that resounded through the world, Tata Steel has slid down the list. A lot of it is connected to its European operations.

Five years after the high profile buyout of Corus — the biggest foreign accession made by an Indian company at $12 billion in those times — Tata Steel is at a crossroads. At 608 pence a share, the price was a 34 per cent premium to Tata Steel's actual offer. Though the deal pelted Tata Steel to the fifth largest steel maker, in hindsight, it looks like an expensive deal.

The Tata Steel group's fortunes have seesawed with steel prices, primarily because the European operations that regard for 60 per cent of earnings do not have locked up raw material coffers, unlike its Indian operations. Jointly, coking coal and iron ore, account for about 65 per cent of the total cost of steel production. Naturally, profitability has slipped over the years. From an enormous amount of ₹12,322 crores at the end of March 2008, Tata Steel's net profit after tax reduction stood at ₹449 crores in 2009 and in 2010 it suffered a loss of ₹2,121 crores. The year 2011 was finally better, worth ₹8,856 crores; but again it declined in 2012, and the price was almost halved to ₹4,949 crores.

Raw ingredients, however, are still a part of the bigger problem. According to some, Corus buys the Rolls-Royce of raw accessories, but with that it is possible to attain records in specific parameters, not gains. It is a combination of factors that affects Tata Steel Europe, raw material apart, similar as under-investment implantations by quondam promoters, and high hand cost, though Tata Steel has lowered significantly, and retardation in Europe.

There are issues with the integration process as well. Ratan Tata had lately said the former British managers of Corus were not prepared to go the extra mile. Whether that has affected the $450 million savings from unification anticipated to be achieved over three years is not known.

Of course, some interned raw material will flow in from Riversdale. Tata Steel is anticipated to receive its first payload of 850,000 tons of coking coal and 200,000 tons of thermal coal from these mines in Mozambique shortly. But for its European operations that have a capacity of about 18 million tons yearly, it could just be a drop in the ocean.

The demand script for Corus does not seen relatively bright either, at least in the near future. According to Tata Steel's assumption, the European economy was believed to contract in 2012, with only borderline growth predicted in 2013. That is not encouraging news for a company which now depends on Europe for 66 per cent of its total product capacity.

So, the focus obviously would be to correct the imbalance and concentrate on India to achieve business growth. The Indian operations are on a steady course, which is poised to grow more once the steel factory at Kaliganagar is commissioned in 2014, though the curriculum is delayed by about five years and Tata Steel is almost sure to miss its target of achieving a capacity of 50 million tons by 2015.

Recently, Ratan Tata observed in his interview to the groups' in-house journal that his involvement in Tata Steel's growth and elaboration has been significant. It appears that his successor will have a lot to unbend in the group flagship.

❑

One Century Foils Another Dismissal

Ratan Tata became the chairman of Tata Motors in 1988; absolutely three years before he took the leadership charge of Tata Sons. Since also, the company has been a patromax for Tata to give chances to his bourns. Be it India's first indigenous car (Tata Indica), first SUV (Safari), first micro truck (Ace) or a Rs 1 lakh car for the common public (Nano), Tata Motors has many firsts to its diary.

The accession of Jaguar Land Rover in 2008 catapulted Tata Motors to one of the world's top transport makers. It has also been an unbelievable monetary success. JLR accounts for nearly two-thirds of profit and 90 per cent of consolidated profit. It also helped the company de-risk its finances from the vagrancies of the marketable vehicle business.

The JLR success, in a way, foils Tata Motors' malfunction to coordinate with Indian car buyers, increasingly changing to its rivals. Fixing this will be top priority for Cyrus Mistry, the new chief, given the quantum of fiscal and strategic capital invested by Tata Sons in the company over the times.

According to the Society of Indian Automobile Manufacturers (Siam), Tata Motors' demanding share in the passenger vehicle segment fell to 12.7 per cent during April-November 2012 from 16.4 per cent in 2006-07. It is India's fourth largest passenger car brand, after Maruti Suzuki, Mahindra & Mahindra and Hyundai.

The decelerating in its domestic business is an economic drag. During the 12 months ending September, the domestic business earned just 5.1 per cent operating profit against 12.5 per cent for its consolidated operations. The fiscal rates of the domestic business are indeed worse, with a return on capital employed (RoCE) of just 3.3 per cent in financial year 2012.

Experts are still not losing hope over Tata's apparent failure in the passenger car market. "At best, it accounts for five per cent of the company's consolidated profit and its financial performance is linked to JLR, followed by its commercial vehicle business in India," says the automobile analyst at a leading brokerage company. Further, he adds, success in the home market matters in the long run, as India is set to feature as one of the world's top vehicle markets in the next 10-15 years.

The Cloud-Free Sky

Experts say the company failed to take advantage of preliminary successes. "Tata Motors is an engineering powerhouse and most of its products have been segment builders. Indica was India's diesel hatchback, Sumo started the MPV (multipurpose vehicle) segment, while Safari pioneered SUVs in India but the company failed to carry it forward," says Pradeep Saxena, executive director, TNS India. He finds an incongruity then. "Brand Tata has certain inherent values embodied in it, such as trust, fairness and integrity. The issue is whether these are good enough for the car category or a buyer cares for another set of values such as modernity, innovation and style," he says.

The poor performance in the domestic car market is recognized by the company, particularly by Ratan Tata himself. "Success in the domestic passenger car market is non-negotiable for us. The goal is to become a strong number two in the near term, and eventually target for the market leadership," says the company's spokesperson.

To achieve this, it will first need to restore Tata Motors' brand image and also submerge the market with new products. "A product is a brand in the auto industry and Tata Motors' product line-up is neither exciting enough or known for being sophisticated and stylish. The company's portfolio hasn't changed much in ten years, except routine product refreshments," says a critic. Others blame the Nano failure; the vehicle consumed funds and operation bandwidth for years. However, "If the Nano had clicked and sold as per the company's expectations, Tata Motors would have been the number two car maker by now," says V.G. Ramakrishnan, director of Frost and Sullivan.

The company's invention machine has braked in recent times. In the seven years from 1991 to 1998, Tata Motors launched five different products — Tata Sierra, Estate, Sumo, Safari and Indica. The pace of new launches has slowed significantly and in the last ten years, it launched just four new products — Indica Vista, Indigo Manza, Nano and Aria, besides renovating age-old models.

Action Required

"When the Indica was first launched in 1998, it was competing against the Maruti Zen and Hyundai Santro. The new generation Indica Vista is up against a dozen or more compact cars. The company needs a breakthrough product and not incremental model changes as it has been doing right through," says Pradeep of TNS India.

The company seems to agree. "There has certainly been a quiet period of late (in terms of new product launches). However, there are new products and offerings in the pipeline," it says.

Experts said it might take time but the company had the means, equipment and infrastructure to make a strong revival. "JLR's acquisition distracted the top management for a while but the domestic market will be its top priority now. JLR's success gives Tata Motors the financial muscle and the engineering prowess to adopt an aggressive posture in India," says the auto analyst at a brokerage house here.

If the company makes the comeback, this will be the finest retirement gift from Cyrus Mistry and the company's top operational circuit to Ratan Tata.

❑

Tata Power: The Global Dimension

Tata Power, the country's largest power mileage in the private sector, would like to forget the year 2012. It had a loss for the first time in over two decades, quite a reversal for a company which not so long ago was a crucial source of growth capital for the entire group. It helped fund the accession of Tata Communications and is a protagonist of the group's telecom adventure, Tata Teleservices. The company remains a heavy megahit in the group, with the third largest balance sheet after Tata Steel and Tata Motors. Ratan Tata became the chairman of Tata Power comparatively late, six years after he became chairman of Tata Sons in 1991.

The company now finds itself during an economic storm, as its biggest investment, on the 4,000 Mw Mundra Ultra Mega Power Design (UMPP) did not go consistent with the intuition. Listed to be completely functional by the middle of the coming year, it will nearly double Tata Power's generating capacity but is rooting a big financial massacre.

The total investment in Mundra accounts for nearly a third of the consolidated means.

When the corporate won the shot to develop the Mundra UMPP, to be grounded on imported coal, this was believed to free Tata Power from the constraints of its regulated business that limited returns from its bread-and-butter power distribution and generation business in the Mumbai region. The company hoped to earn better returns from Mundra through husbandry of scale and energy-effective super-critical technology. It had bid assertively, promising to provide power at ₹2.26 a unit. Comparatively, NTPC, the country's largest driver of coal-fired plants, vended power at a normal of ₹2.66 a unit in FY 2012. The government had imaged imported coal-grounded power plants as domestic force was not suitable to embrace the demand.

Tata Power's computations were grounded on plans to import coal from Indonesia when international prices were around $40 a ton at the time of bidding in 2006. It also bought a 30 per cent equity stake in two major Indonesian thermal coal manufacturers, KPC and PTA, in March 2007. But global coal prices surged past $100 a ton in 2011 and the Indonesian government put up an embargo on exports under the labeled price from September 2011. This made import of coal economically unviable for Tata Power and the Mundra planning is now unfit to make indeed functional profit; it cannot service the project debt on its own.

Coastal Gujarat Power Ltd (CGPL), the special purpose vehicle set up to apply the plan, reported operating losses of Rs 2.3 crores on earnings of Rs 363 crores in the quarter ending September. The total loss, including finance and deprecation cost, was Rs 461 crores. In comparison, the Tata Power standalone business reported an operating contour of 27 per cent in the last quarter.

Urging

Cyrus Mistry, the new chairman of the group, now faces the challenge of satisfying Mundra consumers – six devisee state governments – to agree to a price rise so that the project becomes financially feasible.

CGPL is seeking intervention from the Central Electricity Regulatory Commission for an upward modification in rates to over Rs 3 per unit. "We are hopeful of an early resolution of the issue," said Anil Sardana, managing director, Tata Power.

Global rating agency Standard & Poor's has downgraded Tata Power's long-term rating to 'BB -'. This is an academic and non-investment grade rating. "The outlook revision reflects our expectation that Tata Power's cash flow and financial risk profile could deteriorate over the coming six to nine months because the company has breached a debt-to-equity ratio covenant on loans to its Mundra project," S&P credit analyst Rajiv Vishwanathan observed in a declaration last July.

To alleviate the threat, the company has offered to restructure—it will transfer 75 per cent of its equity interest in Indonesian coal mines to CGPL, so that it uses the dividends from coal to service the debt in the intermediate period.

"To an extent, Tata Power was aware of the risk it was taking on coal prices, so it tried to mitigate it by taking part-ownership of the mines," said Murtuza Arsiwalla, analyst at Kotak Institutional Equities. "But the extreme volatility of coal prices that followed was completely unexpected."

The reversal at Mundra has, still, not dissuaded Tata Power's growth plans or to go laggardly on globalization. It aimed for 26,000 Mw of generation capacity by 2020, by setting up more power plants in India and expanding abroad, to de-risk it from energy dearths and fuel shortage then.

Its non-Mundra business, still, continues to be inflated and is growing at a steady pace. The company enjoys a strong 'AA-' rating standing for its domestic and rupee-denominated borrowing programmes, thanks to its regulated power generation and distribution business. “The rating on Tata Power continues to reflect its strong business position as an integrated power company. Its cash flows from core licensed operations are stable due to the regulated nature of the business,” said Amod Khanorkar, analyst with CARE Ratings in a note recently.

❑

The Defensive Tata

On November 15, 2010, Ratan Tata delivered a lecture on "India in the 21st century: Opportunities and Challenges" in Dehradun, the capital of Uttarakhand. The lecture would have gone overlooked, had Tata not exposed that he thrice tried to get into civil aeronautics but his attempts were unsuccessful because a minister demanded to be paid Rs 15 crores in backhanders and he refused to do so.

"We approached three prime ministers also, but an individual thwarted our efforts to form the airline," he said. "I did not want to go to bed knowing that I set up an airline by paying Rs 15 crores." This demurred up a storm. Some people prompted Tata to name the minister, given the strong anti-corruption statement in the country. Others said there was no point speaking out against the misdemeanour ten years latterly. Yet, it was a rare admission of missed openings in Tata's 20-year-long career as the chairman of Tata Sons.

As he takes stock, Tata will surely feel good about many of his enterprises: the metamorphosis of Tata Steel and

Tata Motors, growth of TCS, expansion of Tata Tea, etc. On the other side, his domestic car business has failed to live up to the original pledge of two high-profile launches (the Indica and Nano), he exited FMCG (Tomco and Lakme) and missed the smash, his casing action is still to attain scale, his pharmaceutical incursion (Advinus) is yet to get into the big league, his telecom companies are way behind the leaders, and his aeronautics plans just could not take shape.

J.R.D. Tata had started India's first industrial airline, Tata Airlines, in the 1930s. After Independence, it was nationalized and renamed Air India. Though the Tata group was out of the airline, the business always remained close to its heart. Some days ago, the central government's newer move opened up the opportunity to organize a reunion of J.R.D. Tata's brightest baby, the Air India, to come back home. In the 1990s, when the sector was opened up for classified companies, Tata knew the time had occurred. He snappily put together an alliance with Singapore Airlines to start a domestic carrier. Also the laws changed overnight. Foreign airlines were barred from retaining even a single share in a domestic carrier. Tata's proposed airline with Singapore Airlines could not take off.

Who obstructed the plans?

Maharaj Kishen Kaw, a former mandarin who was the civil aeronautics clerk when Inder Kumar Gujral was the prime minister (April 1997 to March 1998), in his recent book, *An Outsider Everywhere: Revelations by an Insider*, has said that it was the work of Tata's rivals. "The Tatas had mooted a proposal for a private airline with 40 per cent equity contribution from Singapore Airlines. As this would have been a formidable competitor, Jet Airways tried hard to upset rules regarding foreign equity contribution," Kaw wrote. He said that CM Ibrahim, the then civil aviation minister, was not attracted by the Tata offer. "The minister did not clear the file, despite several attempts on my part," Kaw added. The sector, of course, is stuck in fatalities. It is not sure if the stillborn offer was a blessing in disguise.

Telecom is a different story. Tata Teleservices has 76.7 million subscribers (as of October 31, according to the Telecom Regulatory Authority of India), which puts it in the fifth place after Bharti Airtel (186.4 million), Vodafone (153.1 million), Reliance Communications (134 million) and Idea Cellular (115.7 million). Tata Teleservices, earlier had taken the CDMA route, and not GSM, to mobile telephony. Though largely effective for transmitting data, CDMA suffered from some impediments and stumbling blocks. For instance, the handset came whisked with the service. Secondly, a royalty had to be paid to Qualcomm, the service provider, which eroded the gains. The future was with GSM.

The window of occasion to launch GSM service showed up in 2007 when the department of telecommunications, under Andimuthu Raja, decided to arrange GSM spectrum to CDMA players at a consolidated amount for all of India. Effects went crazy for Tata Teleservices right from the launch.

On October 18, Raja, while approving the trade of crossover spectrum noted on the file that "For allocation of spectrum, the date of payment of the required fee should determine the seniority". Three CDMA service operators, Reliance Communications, Shyam Telelink and HFCL Infotel, had applied for the GSM license in 2006. In principles approval was granted to these three on October 18 itself, though the press release to this effect was only issued the following day. On October 19, Reliance Communications deposited the figure of Rs 1,645 crores (for 20 of the 22 telecom circles) and came right on top of the line for spectrum.

It was distributed spectrum on January 10 and 11, 2008. Tata Teleservices applied on October 20. Now, Raja decided to change the policy and conjoined Tata Teleservices with other campaigners of spectrum. In principle he gave approval to Tata Teleservices's offer only on January 10, 2008, when the company was needed to deposit the license amount. Its operations were entered at DoT's reception counter and further delivered to the office of the wireless counsel. Then, the 'ghosts' appeared, and from there the applications went missing!

On December 8, 2010, Tata wrote to Rajeev Chandraskehar, who had alleged of inaptly grabbing spectrum under the crossover window: "The company (Tata Teleservices) has strictly followed the applicable policy and has been severely disadvantaged, as you are well aware, by certain powerful politically connected operators who have willfully subverted policy under various telecom ministers, which has subsequently been regularized to their advantage. The same operators continue to subvert policy, have even paid the fee for spectrum even before the announcement of policy and have 'de facto ownership' in several new telecom enterprises." Tata Teleservices had not got spectrum in Delhi and some other circles even three years after the advertisement of the policy, Tata added.

So, it is hereby clearly understood, that, in telecom, lobbying and political influences are everything.

❑

Black Mark in the White Clipboard

Ratan Naval Tata's outstanding career as the master of Tata Sons has seen numerous firsts: high-rattle slugfests were one of them. Right through his two-decade long spell as chairman, Tata has in no way nestled down from any challenger or adversity. Known to speak his mind and that too intimately, he has had several run-sways over the times with peers in commercial India, politicians and, of course, media.

His critics say that Tata was not one to overlook possessions in a rush, and call him bigoted. Rajya Sabha member Rajeev Chandrasekhar says, "The Tata group is caught between trying to maximize return on capital employed like any other business groups in India and remaining rooted to doing business that is immorally comfortable".

Here are the instances of some of his home-ground as well as away-ground hurdles:

1. **Battling the Grey hairs:** Soon after J.R.D. Tata made him the chairman of Tata Industries in 1981, four elderly associates decided that they would make life problematic for Ratan Tata.

   That was perhaps an understatement, as what followed would have put even the worst palace schemes to shame. The battle Tata encountered was from Russi Mody at Tata Steel, Darbari Seth at Tata Chemicals, Ajit Kerkar at Indian Hotels and Nani Palkhivala at ACC – people who ran their companies without any hindrance.

   But Tata delivered a masterstroke — the Tata Sons board gave full support to his offer for administering a rule that set 75 as the retirement age for all Tata directors. While this helped the removal of Seth, ill-health whisked Palkhivala's departure. Ajit Kerkar, who desisted to be the executive chairman of Indian Hotels when he turned 65, was of course banished for different reasons.

   It is another matter that Tata himself again changed the retirement rules to continue running the group as the non-executive chairman for another ten springs.

2. **The Telecom Imbroglio:** Telecom has been one of the bitterest hurdles that Tata has overcome. By the time the big bosses – read Tata and Reliance – wanted to get into the business, the nouveau riche were already doing well. From entering the skirmish to selection of technology, Tata fought the GSM atrium tooth and nail. The public slugfest started in 2006, when a commission of the Department of Telecom blazoned its spectrum allocation policy for new technologies like 3G and Wimax. The policy stated that telecom companies would get spectrum depending on the number of consumers they had. With its subscriber base, there was no way that Tata could have aspired for an advanced share of spectrum compared with the rivals.

So Tata wrote letters to J.S. Sarma, the then secretary, Department of Telecom, and Prime Minister Manmohan Singh, suggesting that the additional spectrum should be auctioned as it was a scarce resource.

Whether it is the matter of out-of-turn spectrum allocation or getting fresh spectrum for free, most of these vexing issues have been raised by Tata at different points. Tata has also admitted that he had a "chemistry problem" with ex-telecom minister Dayandhi Maran.

3. **No Tissue to Confront Issue:** Once the power structure receives its holder, the other equal sectors become inevitable opponents in terms of different means. Like telecom, Tata has fought other business houses even in the power sector. And his anathema in this segment is Anil Ambani's power companies.

   Whether it is the battle for consumers in Mumbai or ultra mega power systems, Tata has used the legal system to fight rivals in this space.

   Reliance Infrastructure (erstwhile Reliance Energy) has alleged Tata Power of hooking its guests, while Tata Power sought payment of dues that had collected over a period.

   Tata Power has gone to court on the issue of residue coal by Reliance Power from the interned mines that came with the UMPP.

4. **The Singur Turmoil:** This was definitely one of Ratan Tata's biggest despondencies. The Nano project in West Bengal, ended up as a calamity after the Tatas moved out of the state on October 3, 2008, after Mamata Banerjee's Trinamool Congress started the save cropland movement. Tata eventually left Singur, but not before a public disapprobation of the agitation led by Banerjee. Though the court battle over compensation for the Singur land continues, the two protagonists have more recently sought to mend their shattered relationship through pacific tones in their public statements.

5. **The Tape Issue*:*** What actually put Tata in the eye of the storm were the leaked videotapes that revealed exchanges that his lobbyist and the proprietor of public relations firm, Vaishnavi Communications, Niira Radia, had with media personnel and government officers. After the videotapes caused a public rampage, Tata said that the leaks were to produce a smokescreen around the 2G contestation. He also moved the Supreme Court, questioning the exposure of private exchanges.

❑

The Global Prospect

It took Ratan Tata a full decade to make the group globalized. But it was the proverbial pause before the storm as what followed was some of the most audacious deals that commercial India had seen till they happened.

The group became bolder as well – Tetley was acquired for $450 million; JLR for $2.3 billion and Corus for $12.1 billion.

"I would put Tata in the larger group of 'globalizing' companies, that is, ones that have an international presence but have still not made their presence felt everywhere in the world. Tata is strong in Britain, the US and South Africa, but less high-profile elsewhere," says Morgen Witzel, author of *Tata: The Evolution of a Corporate Brand*.

In terms of sheer figures, its global operations contributed as much as 58 per cent of the $100 billion (Rs 4.75 lakh crores) group's consolidated earnings in 2011-12. For Tata Steel, the share of global operations is as much as 74 per cent; for Tata Global, it is 70 per cent; for Tata Motors, it is 67 per cent and for Indian Hotels, it is 25.77 per cent.

A snap of the companies, which have gone global, reflect a mixed scenario. The return on net worth (RoNW or return on equity) for Tata Global at 8 per cent is more or less the same at the time of acquiring Tetley and now. In case of JLR, it has leaped from negative to a massive 52 per cent. For Indian Hotels, still, it has declined from 14 per cent to lower than a percentage point. And Tata Steel's RoNW has reduced from 37 per cent to 7 per cent.

In fact, Tata Steel Europe is hurting the group poorly. Indeed Ishat Hussain, non-executive director of Tata Sons, in response to a narrative in the *Economist*, recognized Tata Steel's troubles, "The Return on capital employed (RoCE) since 2010 has been highly distorted by the performance of one business: Tata Steel. The RoCE for Tata companies, excluding Tata Steel Europe and the capital work-in-progress of Tata Steel in India, is 14 per cent."

Evidently, a 4 per cent drag on the overall group's RoCE cannot be taken casually.

Though the fiscal sector extremity since 2008 has led to decelerating down of demand from automobile and construction companies – the key consumers of Corus - many say that the deal was precious. Lakshmi Mittal's $34 billion accession of Arcelor in June 2006 was cheaper at EBITDA (earnings before interest, duty, depreciation and amortization) multiple of 4.3 vis-à-vis 9 for Tata Steel's accession of Corus.

That is reflected in the performance of the share price. When the deal was declared on June 30, 2006, Tata Steel's share price stood at ₹473 and market cap at ₹29,516 crores. In November 2012, the respective figures are ₹377 and ₹37,431 crores. The equity base, still, has increased supremely. To patronize the deal, the group issued 390 million shares, raising the equity base from 580 million to 970 million. During a similar period, the sensex shot up 82 per cent while the company's stock price is down 20 per cent.

The value of the accession has eroded considerably. However, which operates in an analogous terrain, their market cap stands at $26 billion, if one considers peers like Arcelor Mittal. Tata Steel, Europe which has one-fifth of Arcelor Mittal's capacity should be valued at $5 billion. In other words, the market value of Tata Steel is lower than the debt ($6 billion) it raised, and half the overall price paid at $12.1 billion. Indeed capacity utilization has fallen to 14 million tons in FY 2011-12 from 23.1 million tons in FY 07-08.

JLR, on the other hand, is a completely different story; however there were primary interruptions which forced Tata Motors to post a loss of ₹2,465 crores in 2008-09. But now, the marquee automobile company is the crown jewel of the group. In fact, if JLR had not paid a dividend of ₹1,312 crores to Tata Motors in the second alternate quarter of the current fiscal time, the parent company would have declared a loss.

Within these two giant deals, there is Tetley which has done relatively well. Witzel says, "The Tetley acquisition seems to have gone very well, partly because Tata Beverages has taken a soft approach to managing it. Most people in the UK still don't know that it is possessed by Tata Beverages." And the figures continue to be stable.

Indian Hotels has suffered the mass of a lackluster world economy. "The international acquisitions done by Indian Hotels have not been earning per share accretive due to economic slowdown leading to lower passenger traffic," said Rashes Shah, analyst with ICICI Securities. With the company willing to go aggressive with the Orient Express deal, the results will only show in 10-20 times, say analysts. The figures, as a result, are not too flattering.

While the jury is still out on how Tata has done in his global gambles, the fact is they have been bold, but not inescapably beautiful.

Tata Global Beverages (TGB) may not be big contributors to the Tata kitty, but are still important to its expansion story. Trent, Tata Global Beverages (TGB), Titan Industries and Tata Chemicals have together grown at a compounded annual growth rate of 23 per cent in the past six years. They continue to be the rising stars in the group with each clocking double-number top line growth. Tata Chemicals grew at a CAGR of close to 23 per cent in the last six times. Trent, Titan and TGB grew by 30 per cent, 35 per cent and 13 per cent independently in the same time frame.

While the four companies contributed just about 7 per cent to the total development of the Tata Group in the 2011-12 financial years, critics say this number could go up as these businesses ride the consumption smash.

Group spectators say that the fabulous four have actually helped the over 100-year-old Tata empire mark its presence in daylight sectors similar to fast-moving consumer goods (FMCG), retail, agric, memoir and nano-technology. It is these sectors amongst its other staple sections of information technology, automotive, hospitality, power and steel that the Tatas are highly counting on as they place themselves as an organization of idealism on the global stage.

It is also from among these very sectors that the Tatas' first major international accession happened.

The time was 2000 and the concurrence was Tetley, a company three times the size of TGB also called Tata Tea, with an allocation of 7 per cent of the world tea demand and ranked number two after Unilever's Brooke-Bond-Lipton. TGB was an original player also largely known for tea and coffee products. Its ingrained play was hardly significant beyond Indian props though the company did have a coordinate venture with Tetley for export of its products. But it demanded a strong platform to launch itself on the global stage. That occasion came with the vast amount (Rs. 1,500 crores) of leveraged buyout of Tetley, the largest overseas accession for an Indian company.

While making the advertisement in February 2000, Chairman Ratan Tata had famously said, "It is a bold move and I hope that other Indian corporates will follow."

They did. But more so it gave the Tatas the courage to take on indeed bigger challenges. That is, acquire further businesses across sectors. In Beverages alone in the last decade, TGB has wrapped up a string of deals including Good Earth and Eight O'clock Coffee in the US, Jemca in the Czech Republic and Grand in Russia.

The company retains its appetite for more, but now says that it would like to concentrate on consolidation and organic growth. "We are a natural Beverages company and our focus will be on tea, coffee and water," Harish Bhat, managing director, TGB, had said in a recent interview with *Business Standard*.

The company is open to striking further alliances with like-minded mates, if needed - it has two at the moment, one with PepsiCo, the other with Starbucks - and is keen to increase its earnings from coffee and water.

But TGB is not the only company where Tatas' global intentions have played out ahead of other sectors in the group.

Titan is another case in point. Established as a common venture between the Tatas and the Tamil Nadu Industrial Development Corporation (TIDCO) in 1984, the company has in the last three decades registered itself not only as a foremost maker of watches in India, but also amongst the pinnacle in the world. It is presently eying the number three position - a jump two places from number five, where it ranks internationally in the watch market.

In India, Titan accounts for about 25 per cent of the volume and 40 per cent of the value of the over 50-million-unit-watch market.

It has also created some adorable brands similar as Fastrack for youth, Raga for women, Nebula, a gold watch targeted at the ultra-expensive customers' end and Sonata at the lower end.

In the last many years, Titan has devoted its attention to other businesses too such as jewellery under Tanishq, which gives it over 70 per cent of its earnings nowadays, and goggles, a new area it ventured into besides leather accessories such as holdalls, belts and bags, as it aims to take advantage of India's consumption and retail smash. Titan's managing director, Bhaskar Bhat, has said that the company will continue looking at all lifestyle accessories barring apparels.

While Titan's growth has been largely driven by organic measures, it has wrapped up many deals like the accession of the Swiss heritage brand Favre-Leuba last time. Enterprise was replete in July this year that it was meaning a $1-billion accession of Canada-grounded luxury watches and jewellery-retailer Harry Winston. But this was negated by the company.

On Trent, the government's move to authorize foreign direct investment in retail has opened up opportunities for a coalition in that part, say analysts. The loss-making company already has a franchise agreement with Tesco under which the Indian firm's Star Bazaar supermarkets use Tesco's supply chains and structure. Both Trent and Tesco are now supposed to be exploring the opportunity of expanding their alliance in the wake of parliament's nod to retail FDI, say sources.

Tata Chemicals, on the other hand, has expanded into three areas: living rudiments, industry rudiments and farm rudiments—from a patron of largely inorganic chemicals such as soda ash, a base component in numerous industries. Under living rudiments come the company's consumer businesses—swab, water, ingrained goods and neutraceuticals. Under industry rudiments, come the core bulk and specialty chemicals and cement, while farm rudiments dwell on crop nutrition and protection and seeds. Company directors say that the metamorphosis from a commodity company to one furnishing complex results in different areas was led by the need to be applicable in changing times. In the last many years, Tata Chemicals has made a series of accessions in inorganic chemicals and has also invested heavily in agribusiness. It is now concentrating its attention on its exploration and development capabilities.

The Nano, master-work of Ratan Tata, has been synonymous with inventions in rising markets. His trouble to fill the white spot between two-wheelers and mini cars for Indian mass family transportation needs has presumably captured the maximum mind space worldwide as an economical engineering success.

The success of Nano was not in just being the cheapest four-wheeler in the world, at Rs 1 lakh at the time of launch. It was the inventions that made the car cheap. The global four-wheeler industry is enthusiastic on modular ways to produce motorcars with different prices and design features. The Nano is erected from modular factors, which can be made and packed independently for assembly at different locales. In effect, the Nano is designed for distribution in accoutrements assembled and serviced by local entrepreneurs globally.

Germany's Roland Berger Strategy Advisers in its lately-released report on global invention shifting to rising markets, says, "Frugal product inventions must start in the company's mindset", recalling Platonic tune of 'imitation' in other words.

This is what Ratan Tata, outgoing chairman of the $100-billion Tata Group, has been driving in the final half of his captaincy of India's largest business empire for over two decades.

This is also the period when Indian companies saw a rush of global competition in the domestic markets. This made consumers discerning, with better products and enhanced client service.

"With globalization, the need for innovation became more critical for Indian companies' survival," says Wilfried Aulbur, managing partner, Roland Berger, who co-authored the report with his other associates. "This led many companies to put more focus on innovation to address new market opportunities," he says.

For case, when Korean auto maker Hyundai Motor set up shop in India in 1996, there were five major auto makers in the country: Maruti Udyog (now, Maruti Suzuki India), Hindustan Motors, Premier Automobiles (now, Premier Ltd), TELCO (now, Tata Motors), and Mahindra & Mahindra (M&M).

Now, Hyundai is the second largest auto maker in India after Maruti Suzuki, still leading the pack. Tata Motors and M&M have been in neck-to-neck competition this time for the third and fourth positions.

But the most distinctive part is that Hindustan Motors and Premier Automobiles are nowhere in the race at present, precisely because of their incapability to innovate and upgrade according to the changing market conditions.

Tata Motors had tasted the changing market condition and it brought out the first indigenous four-wheeler, Indica, in 1999; a small truck, the Ace, in 2005 and the innovative Nano in 2008 to capture new market openings. There are more similar exemplifications from the group, similar as setting up Ginger Budget Hotels in 2002 and making a super computer, Eka, in 2005.

In fact, there have been innumerable cases when the over-a-century-old Tata Group has been an avant-garde. In 1907, Tata Steel became the first Indian company to elevate capital in India. J.R.D. Tata founded Tata Airlines in 1932 and TCS in 1968. Tata Motors made India's first indigenous light marketable vehicle, the Tata 407, in 1986.

Though invention, modification and innovation have been in the group's DNA, the urgency for this became more prominent recently. When the economy-marker first opened in the early 1990s, the group realized its business processes were weak. So, in 1995, it introduced the Tata Business Excellence Model. Any company that uses the Tata brand name or totem has to abide by the model. Under this, companies are given scores out of 1000 every time.

But invention within the group was sporadic. "We had to accelerate and create urgency for the democratization of innovation. This had become more important with the Tata Group going global and the Indian economy getting globalized," said Sunil Sinha, CEO of Tata Quality Management Services (a division of Tata Sons) before.

In 2006, an InnoMission (innovation mission) of 10 Tata Group CEOs went to the US and saw invention at work in companies similar as 3M, Microsoft, Intel, Hewlett-Packard and Raytheon. In the coming time, another project was launched, this time in the other direction, to Japanese companies such as Fuji, Olympus, Toshiba, Nissan and Hitachi. A third undertaking went to Cambridge to traverse the eco-system and to find the scope for innovation there.

The first result was the conformation of Tata Group Innovation Forum (TGIF), commanded to act as a catalyst for invention. It meets every two months (in a different area so that native companies can share) to take stock of the situation and omit hindrances.

The coming step was to honour and award invention within the group InnoVista. These awards are locally acclaimed as well as national. Ratan Tata gives the national awards once a time.

There are three categories: Promising Innovations, The Leading Edge and Dare to Try. An independent jury judges the entries. From 101 from 31 companies in 2006, entries rose to 117 from 39 companies in 2007, also to 289 entries from 47 companies in 2008, and from 62 companies in 2009 to entries from 71 Tata companies in 2012.

The sharp leap in entries from 2009 had a lot to do with the triumphant launch of the Nano. "That fired the imagination of the people in the Tata Group," said R. Gopalakrishnan, administrative director at Tata Sons, before.

After much deliberation, TGIF espoused the Innometer developed by Julian Birkinshaw of the London Business School. It measures the invention process and culture on a scale of zero to five, and can be run on the whole company, a unit or even a small platoon.

Another hedge to invention in the group was that the various Tata companies would not communicate with each other. Ratan Tata, when he became chairman in the early 1990s, removed key chieftains like Russi Mody, Ajit Kerkar and Darbari Seth. A group identity was forged, but collaboration still did not take place. So, TGIF decided to set up InnoClusters— groups of companies that could work jointly in diverse areas.

There are four similar clusters: nanotechnology, plastics and mixes, information technology and water. One of the biggest clusters, of 10 companies, is on nanotechnology. "The Swach water purifier is a perfect example where TCS, Tata Chemicals and Titan came together," said Gopalakrishnan.

Further, the TGIF came with a web-grounded open invention action called InnoVerse. Workers can post a problem on the intranet, to which anybody can give an opinion. People can go on ideas with the 1000 karma points they get.

The group spent $2.7 billion on exploration and development in 2010-11, about three per cent of its development in that time. So, has the Tata Group changed? It is still early days, says Gopalakrishnan. "It's not as if there is a storm gathering; it's just some rain here and there."

From a group run by satraps, the outgoing chairman of Tata group, Ratan Tata, will be credited with founding a youthful platoon of CEOs to run their concerned companies, giving them a free hand as long as they followed the introductory principles of ethics, values and commercial governance. Tata hired the best competent talents from across the world as he saw beforehand on that to survive in the wake of profitable liberalization, Indian companies demanded to go global and borrow superlative practices.

Backed by a trusted team A, led by fellow Tata Sons director R.K. Krishna Kumar, Tata led the metamorphosis by handing over unconnected businesses such as cosmetics, detergents and cement — ranking numerous satraps close to precursor J.R.D. Tata. The group rather concentrated on new generation businesses such as telecom, software, retail and cars.

Tata formed a network of youthful CEOs, now in their 40s and running their separate companies efficiently. This includes Karl Slym, hired from General Motors to run Tata Motors after the Nano project was unsuccessful to make a profitable amount of money. There were other youngster fighters as well, such as: Brotin Banerjee, 36, who heads Tata Housing Development Company; N Chandrasekharan, 48, CEO of TCS; Anil Sardana, 52, of Tata Power; N. Srinath, 49, of Tata Teleservices, and R. Mukundan, 44, CEO of Tata Chemicals.

Although Tata encountered a tough time in his career, thanks to the public fight with Russi Mody and Ajit Kerkar, he managed to ease out the satraps and succeeded in receiving his own people at the rudder of every provision.

According to Tata Group interposers, it was Kumar who was necessary in setting up the race commission for Tata and helped set the retirement age of Tata directors to get around any Russi Mody occasion in future. When Ratan Tata was under siege from Mody, the then chairman of Tata Steel and Kerkar, the then chairman of Indian Hotels, the operators of Taj Hotels, and Darbari Seth of Tata Chemicals, it was Kumar who played an important part in the ouster of the satraps.

Since also, Tata and Kumar have led the transition of the group from a regulatory set up to a nimble-footed group, which is now earning half of its $100-billion earnings from its overseas operations. In a recent interview with *Business Standard*, Kumar said the aggressive combinations and accessions policy of the group is now eventually giving dividends. "Just look at the JLR; we are now earning every quarter what we spent on buying the company," he said. In 2012, JLR made an over-profit on a profit of about Rs 1.16 lakh crores.

In Tata Chemicals, R. Mukundan is navigating the company towards specialty chemicals and consumer products, as customers insist on change along with increasing expenditure. “As India becomes more urbanized and as income situations and habits change, the country’s GDP will rise and supply chains will shift; there will be demand for new types of chemicals and products,” says Mukundan. As Tata Steel Managing Director H.M. Nerurkar is due to retire beforehand coming time, interposers say a hunt is already on for the coming MD. Among the frontal runners is 44-year-old Kaushik Chatterjee, the CFO of Tata Steel, who helped the company restructure its debt taken to fund its accession abroad of Corus.

As Kumar is also retiring from Tata Sons and group companies by July coming time, Tata’s new chairman Cyrus Mistry will be starting his innings with a fresh line up. This will help the new chairman to make his own platoon. With Tata promising every help to his successor, it will be now over to Mistry to take the Tata Group to a better and more profitable extent.

❑

The Relay Race Continues

In August 2010, Ratan Tata announced that he would be retiring as the group chairman in December 2012. He earlier already took retirement in 2012 from all the executive positions he had been into abide by the group's retirement policy of announcing it at the age of 65. He was at the age of his official retirement in 2007 (when he turned 70 years), but the board of Tata Sons modified the policy and extended the retirement age of non-executive directors to 75 years that permitted him to continue as the head of the Tata group.

Over the years, when talking about his retirement, Ratan Tata had said he would prefer a person in his 40s or early 50s to replace him as that would give the new chairman a long term. To avoid the contradictions that he had to go through in 1991, he set up a five-member hunt commission – consisting of Tata Sons directors, R.K. Krishna Kumar and Cyrus Mistry, who is the son of Shapoorji Pallonji Mistry, the largest individual shareholder in Tata Sons; Noshir Soonawala, former vice chairman of Tata Sons; Shirin Bharucha, group legal counsel and Warwick University

Professor, Lord Kumar Bhattacharyya – to find the group's coming chairman. The commission was given an open accreditation to find the right seeker, who could be within or outside the Tata group, an Indian public or a non-Indian. Several known names were considered, with Noel Tata, being acceptable by many as the likely victor. Noel Tata was not only Ratan Tata's half-brother, but also Shapoorji Pallonji Mistry's son-in-law. He was the Vice Chairman of Trent Ltd. and the Managing Director of Tata International.

Anyway, the commission which had primarily set itself a deadline of March 2011 to find a successor attempted to find a suitable and competent seeker. R.K. Krishna Kumar said, "Our committee has come to the conclusion that we cannot find a replacement for Mr. Tata! We may have to change and rearrange the model in terms of what we are looking for. It is not an easy task, but we will identify the next chairman of Tata Sons within a few weeks by the end of May or early June."

Eventually, on November 23, 2011, the hunt commission recommended Cyrus Mistry, its former member who had recued himself from the commission in early 2011, as the coming Tata group chairman. Mistry, an alumnus of Imperial College, London (Engineering), and London Business School (Management), had been a member of the board of Tata Sons since 2006.

Describing the choice as a "good and far-sighted one", Ratan Tata said, "I have been impressed with the quality and calibre of his participation, his astute observations and his humility. Don't be fooled by his quiet demeanour. He is his own person, knows where he wants to be. I feel confident that he will lead the group in a manner that is of the highest quality. Cyrus is the right person for the job, I welcome him."

Though this selection could not avoid the difficulties in acceptance as the social media and virtual world had a significant impact not only on professional agenda but on personal aspects too. Dismissing sundries that his larger-than-life persona would prevaricate or temporize after he retired, Ratan Tata said, "I don't think it is right to have a ghost to shadow over somebody" and his advice to Mistry was, "you should be your own person, you should take your own call and you should decide what you want to".

Accepting the responsibility, Cyrus Mistry said, "...the responsibility of Chairmanship brings with it the winds of change, but the core of the Tata Group must and will remain unchanged. Our commitment to maintaining the highest ethical standard in the conduct of our enterprises; our continuous emphasis on business excellence and managerial competence; our belief in our employees and their well-being; our sense of obligation to the customers we serve; our responsibilities towards the environment and the communities that we touch and the greater good of the countries we operate in – without this core DNA that is uniquely Tata, there is nothing to differentiate us from our peers.

The Tata Group's revenue today stands at over $100 billion. That seems an incredible figure when you consider where we were a decade ago. With our collaborative zeal and effort, I am convinced that we can together write a future that continues to build on the past and takes the Tata name to newer frontiers of growth. "

❑

The Policy Differs, Not the Kingdom, Nor The King

Unlike his precursor, J.R.D. Tata, who in 1991 handed over to him the chairmanship of Tata Sons as well as control of the trusts, Ratan Tata will continue to retain control of the second. It is noteworthy, that, there is no retirement age at the trusts, which together control around 66 per cent of the shares of Tata Sons.

But what will keep Tata really busy in his new office at Elphinstone Building are his mega plans for the trusts, which so far attracted only half his attention. The first suggestion of that came in his acceptance speech for a Lifetime Achievement Award introduced by the Rockefeller Foundation when he said his "life's work isn't done yet" as he has not been able to touch multitudes at the bottom of the class structure in society.

Tata easily believes "patchwork philanthropy" — giving a bit of cloth here and food there — would not go far. So he had moved down relatively beforehand from a donatordependent model from a cooperation model. The alternate part of that drive would come now as Tata does not follow the common belief that charitable institutions have to operate on a hay budget and does not need to produce a professionally-run commercial body.

In a recent interview to American TV intelligencer Charlie Rose, Tata laid out at least a part of his blue-print. He said that he would concentrate on pastoral development, conservation of water and his most important aim is to do better in nutrition for children and pregnant women.

That is a long enough list. But does it mean he would cut himself off absolutely from all that is ever considered marketable in nature? The answer is a big No. Just like JRD, he would remain Chairman Emeritus of Tata Sons and a number of other associate group companies – an ornamental designation — but one which provides him the moral authority to offer advice if asked for by the new Chairman. Tata himself has made it clear that he would be available to anyone seeking his advice but would refrain from taking any active part in the handling of the group's businesses.

Going by the extraordinary closeness he shares with Cyrus Mistry, the latter would not be abashed or hesitate in seeking his counsel. The advice would clearly be much more frequent in matters relating to Tata Motors. The company, which is absolutely closest to Tata's heart, is suddenly feeling the pressure from newer challengers like Mahindra & Mahindra because of an indifferent performance in domestic markets. Tata has also made no secret desire to remain engaged with the Nano. Going by his public statements, Tata would obviously attempt to reverse that indeed after he retires as he has himself said he would like to be "involved" instead of plan-chalking this is often the position that Nano deals can be. And also there is the buzz about Tata planning to set up a transnational centre with state-of-the-art installations to design a wide range of products. The project centre would be relatively close to his heart as Tata has often said that the one benefit of studying in the School of Architecture was that it tutored him to fiddle when exhausted. He said board meetings were one place he would get tired – that coercion, thankfully, has just got over.

All this is quite a sprinkle for people too junior in age and in the florescence of their working life. But Tata would do some extra. For instance, he has formerly said he would like to attend the annual general meetings of Tata group companies as a shareholder and ask questions. Further, Tata will continue to be on the board of directors of Alcoa, apart from being on the international advisory boards of Mitsubishi, the American International Group, JP Morgan Chase, Rolls Royce, Temasek Holdings and the Monetary Authority of Singapore. He is also on the board of trustees of Cornell University and the University of Southern California.

❑

The Fantasy Breakdown

In one of the most dramatic incidents in recent history, the board of directors of Tata Group on October 24, 2016 suggested for the retrenchment of its chairman Cyrus Mistry with immediate effect and made Ratan Tata the interim chairman, and in February 2017, Mistry was removed as a chairman for Tata Sons. The National Company Law Appellate Tribunal (NCLAT) had decided in December 2019 that the removal of Cyrus Mistry as the Chairman of Tata Sons was illegal and that he should be restored. India's Supreme Court heard an appeal by the $111-billion Empire to quash the NCLAT order that directed the Tata group to rehire the man it fired as chairman. Ratan Tata is tête-à-tête leading the charge in the case, and filed a separate solicitation challenging the ruling in the Supreme Court. The Supreme Court has stayed the NCLAT order that permitted Cyrus Mistry to be restored as Tata Sons' chairman in January 2020. Still the Supreme Court upheld the redundancy of Cyrus Mistry. Ratan Tata made a comeback, taking over the company's interim master for four months. On January 12, 2017, Natarajan Chandrasekharan was suggested as the chairman of Tata Sons, a step he assumed in February 2017.

❑

The Marks Unmarked

Ratan Tata had to face public embarrassment in 2010 when his private exchanges with Niira Radia got publicized on the electronic media. Next time he had to lose face was when the Tata Group forced Cyrus Mistry to abdicate as Chairman, presumably at the asseveration of Ratan Tata. Critics said, ironically, Ratan Tata had brought Cyrus Mistry as his successor with considerable fanfare. Apart from these two difficulties, professional life of Ratan Tata has been without any mark. He has in no way been plant deficient in his conduct as Chairman of the Tata Group or earlier as hand of the Tata Group companies.

❑

The Current Perusal

Tata invested personal savings in Snapdeal – one among India's leading e-commerce websites –and, in January 2016, Teabox, a web premium Indian tea seller, and CashKaro.com, a reduction coupons saver and cash-back website. He has made small investments in both early and late stage companies in India, like Rs 0.95 crores in Ola Cabs. In April 2015, it was reported that Tata had acquired a stake in Chinese smartphone company Xiaomi. In 2016, he invested in Nestaway, a web portal to seek out fully furnished flats for bachelors who later acquired Zenify to start out family rental segment and online pet care portal, Dogspot. Tata Motors unraveled the primary batch of Tigor Electric Vehicles from its Sanand Plant in Gujarat, regarding which Ratan Tata said, "Tigor indicates a willingness to fast-forward India's electric dream. The government has set an ambitious target to possess only electric cars by 2030."

❑

Philanthropist Tata

Tata is a strong devotee of education, pharmaceuticals and rural development, and considered as one of the leading philanthropists in India. Tata backed-up the University of New South Wales Faculty of Engineering to develop capacitive deionization to supply better water to marginal areas.

Tata Hall at the University of California, San Diego (UC San Diego), opened in November 2018, offers facilities for the biological and physical sciences and is the home of the Tata Institute for Genetics and Society. The Tata Institute for Genetics and Society, although a bi-national institution, coordinates the research-programme between UC San Diego and research operations in India to help in societal and infrastructure development within the area of battling vector-borne diseases. Tata Hall is known as in recognition of a generous $70 million from Tata Trusts.

Tata Education and Development Trust, a humanitarian undertaking of Tata Group, endowed a $28 million Tata Scholarship Fund which will allow Cornell University to supply aid to undergraduate students from India. The scholarship fund will support approximately 20 scholars at any given time and can ensure that the absolute best Indian students to get access to Cornell, irrespective of their financial conditions. The scholarships are going to be awarded annually; recipients will have the opportunity of the scholarship for the duration of their undergraduate study at Cornell.

In 2010, Tata Group companies and Tata charities donated $50 million for the development of an executive centre at Harvard Business School (HBS). The head quarter has been named Tata Hall, after Ratan Tata (AMP '75), chairman emeritus of Tata Sons. The entire construction costs are estimated at $100 million. Tata Hall is founded within the northeast corner of the HBS campus, and is dedicated to the Harvard Business School's mid-career Executive Education programme. It is seven storeys tall, and about 155,000 gross square feet. It houses approximately 180 bedrooms, additionally to academic and multi-purpose spaces.

Tata Consultancy Services (TCS) has given the loftiest ever donation by a corporation to Carnegie Mellon University (CMU) for a facility to research in cognitive systems and autonomous vehicles. TCS donated $35 million for this grand 48,000 square-foot building that is called TCS Hall.

In 2014, Tata Group endowed the Indian Institute of Technology, Bombay and formed the Tata Centre for Technology and Design (TCTD) to develop design and engineering principles and equipment suited to the requirements of individuals and communities with limited resources. They gave ₹950 million to the institute which was the highest ever donation received in its history.

Tata Trusts, under the Chairmanship of Ratan Tata, provided a grant of ₹750 million to the Centre for Neuroscience, Indian Institute of Science to review mechanisms determining the causes, symptoms for Alzheimer's disease and to evolve methods for its early diagnosis and treatment. This grant was to be propagated 5 years starting in 2014.

Tata Group, under the leadership of Ratan Tata, formed the MIT Tata Centre of Technology and Design at Massachusetts Institute of Technology (MIT) with a mission to deal with the challenges of resource-constrained communities, with a primary specialization in India.

❑

A Successful Leader

The leadership style of Ratan Tata is deeply embedded in Indian morality. Ratan Tata served the Tata Group for nearly 50 years. He has been relatively active indeed after relinquishing his position as Chairman of the Tata Group in 2012. He is now focusing on the charitable arms of the Tata Group. Infact, he has also turned an angel investor and adroit capital financier. He has supported a number of launch-ups in recent history. Ratan Tata has also been awarded the Padma Vibhushan (2008) and Padma Bhushan (2020)—the Government of India's third and alternate loftiest civilian awards.

Several factors have made Mr. Tata what he is now; some of his Success Mantras are:

1. **Conforming to Life:** Mr. Tata though born and raised in an illustrious family, saw what no child should see, i.e. separation of his parents. Yet he acclimatized well growing up with his grandparents. While he was in the US, he did not live a lavish life. On his return to India, he understood the value of the occasion to take part in

the family business, when J.R.D. Tata insisted that he should not return abroad, giving up his intentions in a way to continue his dream job at IBM. Latterly, after having made NELCO a profit-making unit, all the loss-making units were transferred to him. The world saw the mastery of Mr. Tata when all the loss-making companies handed over to him started performing well. He has proved that in the course of life, there are numerous ups and downs. The need, still, is to snappily acclimatize to those changes and make the best out of oneself and the situation, to bring success and passion in the pursuit of life.

2. **Morality:** Mr. Tata was raised by his grandmother, and she indoctrinated a sense of discipline in him. J.R.D. Tata saw this efficiency in practice yielding good consequences. Therefore, he was made the chairman in 1991. Still, also Tata Group would have been in decline, if he were a man of casual attitude and flexible principles. For instance, when Bill Ford tried to affront Mr. Tata, he was determined to take sweet vengeance by proving to the world that Tata Motors demanded no mercy. This negative occasion of his life further strengthened him in no way to vend out any Tata unit; for this, he ensured that the best practices were followed among the workers and employers.

3. **Good Will and Determination:** Mr. Tata always took pride in the heritage of his group. He never displayed any pride or showed off what he has got. He is a lone man with no family and lives with two dogs, offers sanctum to slapdash dogs in bad rainfall. This is the good will that he carries with himself. In every testing or grueling time in his life, he has never given up, and the result is, under his term of chairmanship earnings grew 40 pack and profit by 50 times. If one can learn from him not to give up and keep following the integral path of good will in particular and professional life, finally its results can be phenomenal.

4. **Thinking for Workers:** The Tata Group and Mr. Tata especially, always understood that workers could make or break the company. They offer their diligence, time, energy, and enthusiasm because of which the group functions. Therefore, one reason for his success is the fact that when it comes to offering gratuities and weal to workers, they follow the most excellent practices. It is to the extent to maintain satisfaction and happiness situations in them to ensure the best productivity rates. It fulfills the integral aspect of running the Tata Group, i.e. broader philanthropic weal through a qualitative change in people's lives.

5. **Learning from the West:** Mr. Tata followed the principle that worked the best for Tata Group, i.e. learning from the West. Mr. Tata was apprehensive in the post-liberalization period and rising privatization, the competition would come through the channels of globalization. He ensured that the best wisdom and technology was used to intensify camaraderie and produce quality products. He invested heavily on the subject of invention and it is this subject that has driven the change under the period of Mr. Tata making him all the way more successful, so much that today every Indian takes pride to enjoy the luxury and comfort of a five star rated Global NCAP buses, which is over and further all the safety parameters of security quested by the Government of India.

❑

Final Words

The mission and aim of the Tata group has always been to advance India's progress by new and modernized means and introduction of technological support through industrialization. Whenever the dictator changes, people were sure that the reign would not change, as every chairperson will continue the former's legacy through efficiency and competence. Ratan Tata, the iconic maestro, was no exception. Right from facing challenges at initial stages to handle the hurdles aroused from home-grounds, making the in-house persons convinced to expand the business worldwide, following the glorious paths of his superlative precursors like Jamsetji Tata, R.D. Tata and obviously his favourite Jeh (J.R.D. Tata). He not only successfully carried forward the baton; he rejuvenated it with new ornaments and set up a velvet-turf for his upcoming successors, creating a pinnacle of glory in his own hand. Even if he does not actively play a role, abiding by the strict rules and regulations of Tata group, his umbrella will always be there to encourage and take India industrially to the golden gate of paradise. ❑

Top Motivational Quotes/Inspiring

1. Always deliver more than expected.
2. Apart from values and ethics which I have tried to live by, the legacy I would like to leave behind is a very simple one - that I have always stood for what I consider to be the right thing, and I have tried to be as fair and equitable as I could be.
3. At Tatas, we believe that if we are not among the top three in an industry, we should look seriously at what it would take to become one of the top three players or think about exiting the industry.
4. Banana republics are run on cronyism.
5. Britain needs a real push. It needs nationalism. The sort of spirit that appears during a war.
6. Business needs to go beyond the interest of their companies to the communities they serve.
7. Challenges need to be given to an organization.
8. Chase the vision, not the money, the money will end up following you.
9. Companies that do not will undoubtedly die.
10. Don't play games that you don't understand, even if you see lots of other people making money from them.
11. Don't take too much advice. Most people who have a lot of advice to give — with a few exceptions — generalize whatever they did. Don't over-analyse everything.
12. Every time we launch a feature, people shout at us.

13. Everyone thinks only about his profit.
14. Get big quietly, so you don't tip off potential competitors.
15. Governance is an important thing, not an application where it suits one so, to micro-control where it suits them on the other hand.
16. Having said that, I hope that a hundred years from now we will spread our wings far beyond India.
17. I admire very successful people. But if that success has been achieved through too much ruthlessness, then I may admire that person, but I can't respect him.
18. I am proud of my country. But we need to unite to make a unified India, free of communalism and casteism.
19. I came seriously close to getting married four times, and each time I backed off in fear or for one reason or another. Each occasion was different, but in hindsight when I look at the people involved, it wasn't a bad thing what I did. I think it may have been more complex had the marriage taken place.
20. I do not know how history will judge me, but let me say that I've spent a lot of time and energy trying to transform the Tatas from a patriarchal concern to an institutional enterprise.
21. I don't believe in taking right decisions.
22. I followed someone who had very large shoes. He had very large shoes. Mr. J.R.D. Tata. He was a legend in the Indian business community. He had been at the helm of the Tata organization for 50 years. You were almost starting to think he was going to be there forever.
23. I have always been very confident and very upbeat about the future potential of India. I think it is a great country with great potential.
24. I have been constantly telling people to encourage people, to question the unquestioned and not to be ashamed to bring up new ideas, new processes to get things done.

25. I have two or three cars that I like, but today, Ferrari would be the best car I have driven in terms of being an impressive car.
26. I may have hurt some people along the way, but I would like to be seen as somebody who has done his best to do the right thing for any situation and not compromised.
27. I take decisions and then make them right.
28. I think the environment has become more competitive. That has made the Indian industry more concerned with a) its customers, b) the quality of its products, and c) its brand image in the marketplace.
29. I think the Tata Group's greatest contribution to the growth of the Indian economy and Indian industry probably happened in the pre-independence era.
30. I think there are many honest businessmen.
31. I think you can have certain specific rules for engaging with India... for example, not allowing mineral resources to be taken out of the country... but there is not a shred of doubt in my mind that when you open an economy you should do it in totality.
32. I will certainly not join politics.
33. I would like to be remembered as a clean businessman who has not partaken in any twists and turns beneath the surface, and one who has been reasonably successful.
34. I would say that one of the things I wish I could do differently would be to be more outgoing.
35. I, for one, am not the kind who loves dwelling on the 'I'.
36. Ideas are easy. Implementation is hard.
37. If history remembers me at all, I hope it will be for this transformation.
38. If it stands the test of public scrutiny, do it... if it doesn't stand the test of public scrutiny then don't do it.
39. If people like you, they'll listen to you, but if they trust you, they'll do business with you.

40. If there are challenges thrown across, then some interesting, innovative solutions are found. Without challenges, the tendency is to go on the same way.
41. If you are not embarrassed by the first version of your product, you've launched too late.
42. If you want to walk fast, walk alone. But if you want to walk far, walk together.
43. If you're interested in the living heart of what you do, focus on building things rather than talking about them.
44. If your actions inspire others to dream more, learn more, do more and become more, you are a leader.
45. India has probably lost its position to China as the world's workshop. At the same time, it has the power to be ahead of China when it comes to knowledge. Not that the Chinese are far behind. They will get there.
46. Indian car buyers have not been exposed to customer care in a competitive environment.
47. IT and the entire communications business have the greatest growth potential. But if you're talking about sheer size, the steel and auto industries will remain at the top.
48. It needs people really to want to see the UK sitting again, maybe not as a colonial power, but as an economic power.
49. It would, therefore, be a mark of failure on my part if it were perceived that Ratan Tata epitomizes the Group's success.
50. It's not about ideas. It's about making ideas happen.
51. I've never believed protectionism of that kind will lead us anywhere.
52. Jardine is the largest dealer of Mercedes in the world. They also sell cars for two or three Japanese makers.
53. Make every detail perfect and limit the number of details to perfect.
54. Modesty is necessary, even if there is also a need for a certain amount of national pride. When it comes down

to it, we have managed our country's economy poorly for long enough.

55. My concern is that the government doesn't appear to care about manufacturing.
56. No one can destroy iron, but its rust can! Likewise, no one can destroy a person, but its mindset can!
57. Nothing works better than just improving your product.
58. One hundred years from now, I expect the Tatas to be much bigger than it is now. More importantly, I hope the Group comes to be regarded as being the best in India... best in the manner in which we operate, best in the products we deliver and best in our value systems and ethics.
59. One of the weaknesses of the Indian industry is that in many areas... like consumer goods... it is very fragmented. Individually, companies might not be able to survive.
60. Our challenge is to invest sufficiently in education.
61. People of great power wield great power, but people of lesser power or people who have fallen out of power go to jail without adequate evidence, or their bodies are found in the trunks of cars.
62. People still believe what they read is necessarily the truth.
63. Power and wealth are not two of my main stakes.
64. Some foreign investors accuse us of being unfair to shareholders by using our resources for community development. Yes, this is money that could have made for dividend payouts, but it also is money that's uplifting and improving the quality of life of people in the rural areas where we operate and work. We owe them that.
65. Some people dream of success, while other people wake up every morning and make it happen.
66. Take the stones people throw at you, and use them to build a monument.

67. The country is now universally recognized as a nation on the move and takes its place amongst the successful economies in the region.
68. The day I am not able to fly will be a sad day for me.
69. The early Rockefellers made their wealth from being in certain businesses and remained personally very wealthy. Tata's were different in the sense the future generations were not so wealthy. They were involved in the business but most of the family wealth was put into the trust and most of the family did not enjoy enormous wealth.
70. The fastest way to change yourself is to associate with people who are already the way you want to be.
71. The foreign investment adds a sense of competition; we should see this as a wake-up call to modernize and upgrade.
72. The future potential is enormous but the country's destiny is in our hands.
73. The government should do its job. The government's job is to run the country, to manage the country, to govern the country.
74. The Group's investments in industries such as steel, textiles, power and hotels were certainly driven by an entrepreneurial spirit, but they were driven, even more, I think, by a desire to make India self-sufficient and independent of its colonial masters then.
75. The political system of the People's Republic of China can make things easy. Decisions are made quickly and results come quickly, too. In our democracy (in India), on the other hand, such things are extremely difficult.
76. The strong live and the weak die. There is some bloodshed, and out of it emerges a much leaner industry, which tends to survive.
77. The Telco is committed to commercial vehicles, where it is bound to remain a major player. What may well

happen in the future is we may split the company into two business units.

78. The time has come for performance to be measured and for allocated funds of the government to reach the people for whom they were intended.
79. The time has come to move from small increments to bold, large initiatives.
80. The time has come to stretch the envelope and set goals which were earlier not seen to be possible.
81. The value of an idea lies in using it.
82. There are many things that, if I have to relive, maybe I will do it another way. But I would not like to look back and think about what I have not been able to.
83. There is no reason to now think that we can conquer the world.
84. Ups and downs in life are very important to keep us going because a straight line even in an ECG means we are not alive.
85. We can be a truly great nation if we set our sights high and deliver to the people the fruits of continued growth, prosperity and equal opportunity.
86. We have provinces, we have the rule of law, and we have a system of justice. But those are also weaknesses when compared with China. On the other hand, one of our strengths is that we are very individualistic, and as individuals, we are very creative. But that, too, is a weakness, because it keeps us from working well together.
87. We like to say that India has the advantage of being a large market.
88. We live in a highly competitive world and we Indians have to struggle to catch up.
89. We need to build India into a land of equal opportunities for all.

90. We need to stop taking baby steps and start thinking globally. It seems to be helping.
91. We're responsible for the fortunes of the company but this is a bone-dry situation in terms of access to credit. Nobody can operate on that basis unless you have large cash balances, which we don't.
92. What are the crumple zones on scooters? The helmet is the only crumple zone I can think of.
93. What do you need to start a business? Three simple things: know your product better than anyone, know your customer, and have a burning desire to succeed.
94. What I have done is to establish growth mechanisms, play down individuals and play up the team that has made the companies what they are.
95. What I would like to do is to leave behind a sustainable entity of a set of companies that operate in an exemplary manner in terms of ethics, values and continue what our ancestors left behind.
96. What is needed is a consortium of companies in one industry, presenting a strong front to the multinationals. The Swiss watch industry did this.
97. When you find an idea that you just can't stop thinking about, that's probably a good one to pursue.
98. When you see in places like Africa and parts of Asia abject poverty, hungry children and malnutrition around you, and you look at yourself as being people who have well-being and comforts, I think it takes a very insensitive, tough person not to feel they need to do something.
99. Wonder what your customer wants? Ask. Don't tell.
100. Young entrepreneurs will make a difference in the Indian ecosystem.

❑

Bibliography

1. Ratan Tata Legacy—An eBook Compilation of reports published in *Business Standard* (dated: December 8, 2012, December 24, 2012, December 25, 2012, December 26, 2012, December 27, 2012, December 28, 2012).
2. *Leading the Tata Group* (A): *The Ratan Tata Years*, by K.S. Manikandan, K. Rajyalakshmi and J. Ramachandran.
3. *Infallibility of Ratan Tata: A Case Study* by Shweta Jha.
4. *Success Principles of Ratan Tata* by Abhishek Kumar.
5. *Beyond the Last Blue Mountains* by R.M. Lala.
6. *Ratan Tata*_Wikipedia.

❑